PRO-CHOICE
AND CHRISTIAN

PRO-CHOICE AND CHRISTIAN

Reconciling Faith, Politics, and Justice

KIRA SCHLESINGER

WESTMINSTER
JOHN KNOX PRESS
LOUISVILLE · KENTUCKY

First edition
Published by Westminster John Knox Press
Louisville, Kentucky

18 19 20 21 22 23 24 25 26—10 9 8 7 6 5 4 3 2

Book design by Drew Stevens
Cover design by Mary Ann Smith

Library of Congress Cataloging-in-Publication Data
Names: Schlesinger, Kira, author.
Title: Pro-choice and Christian : reconciling faith, politics, and justice /
    Kira Schlesinger.
Description: First edition. | Louisville, KY : Westminster John Knox Press,
    [2017] | Includes bibliographical references. |
Identifiers: LCCN 2017013702 (print) | LCCN 2017034892 (ebook) |
    ISBN 9781611648324 (ebk.) | ISBN 9780664262921 (pbk. : alk. paper) |
Subjects: LCSH: Abortion—Religious aspects—Christianity. | Abortion—
    United States.
Classification: LCC HQ767.25 (ebook) | LCC HQ767.25 .S36 2017 (print) |
    DDC 261.8/36—dc23
LC record available at https://lccn.loc.gov/2017013702

CONTENTS

CONTENTS

INTRODUCTION

I never intended to write a book about abortion, but in 2015, I wrote a piece for *Ministry Matters* on how the pro-choice stance that I had held for a long time had become more nuanced and complicated. That article received a lot of hits, a lot of shares, and a lot of nasty comments from fellow Christians, though others expressed appreciation for my viewpoint that went beyond the usual simplistic divisions. At that point in time, it was the scariest and also the most satisfying thing I had written.

Amid the vitriol I received about condoning the murder of unborn children, that piece seemed to hit a nerve with an audience that was uncomfortable with policing the bodies of women but also saw a new life, at whatever stage, as a valuable gift. If pressed, these people would likely fall under the category of "pro-choice," but they were unlikely to attend a rally for Planned Parenthood. At the same time, there were also those who identified more closely with the "pro-life" label, who also saw a new life as a gift, but hesitated to criminalize or condemn women making difficult personal decisions.

What about those of us in the middle who, as Christians, value the gift of life but believe there is a difference between a just-fertilized egg and a fetus at thirty or forty weeks' gestation? What about those of us who see the harmful impact of abortion restrictions on those already living on a razor's edge, trying to make ends meet, and so support a woman's access to abortion *because of* our Christian values of caring for the most vulnerable, not *in spite of* them? Polling tells us that the beliefs of the majority fall somewhere between wanting to see *Roe v. Wade* overturned, abortion criminalized, and women jailed, at one end, and wanting what some politicians have called "unlimited abortion on demand," at the other. Unfortunately, you wouldn't know that the people in this majority exist, because the loudest, most extreme voices dominate the conversation in the media, with both sides vilifying one another and hurling heinous accusations.

In the recent past, it has looked as if the lines were drawn in the sand quite clearly: pro-life vs. pro-choice, Republican vs. Democrat, the right to life of the unborn vs. the right to privacy of the woman, a Christian (meaning Catholic or conservative evangelical) culture of life vs. a secular, individualistic culture of death. We heard little from those who did not fit neatly into these divisions. But people are complicated, and even in the history of this argument over abortion, the lines blur.

Catholic women get abortions at the same rate as other women, and the Catholics for Choice advocacy group makes a robust case for freedom of choice and access to reproductive care from within the Catholic tradition. There are pro-life Democrats who continue the tradition of pre–*Roe v. Wade* pro-life activism by defending the unborn out of a desire to ensure the rights of the most vulnerable. As the demographics of the United States shift and racial and ethnic minorities are projected to become a majority, these categories that make such a neat and tidy media narrative will continue to shift. For example, the Latino/a demographic is predominantly Catholic and pro-life but tends to side with the Democratic Party on immigration issues.

Meanwhile, the liberal factions of mainline Christian denominations have remained strangely silent on abortion, while taking strong stands on other controversial issues, ceding the conversation on abortion to Catholics and evangelicals. Churches continue publicly to debate LGBTQ inclusion and same-sex marriage, and many are very active on a variety of other social justice issues. Clergy and church leadership have boldly declared that Black Lives Matter and have stood against the Dakota Access Pipeline going through Sioux reservation land. Issues of environment, economic inequality, or gender inequality get plenty of airtime. But bring up abortion, and all you hear are crickets. Even within so-called progressive Christianity, abortion is a third-rail topic, untouchable in conversation or from the pulpit. In denominations like the United Methodist Church that contain a variety of viewpoints, on abortion there has been a move to the right at the highest levels of church governance. While many denominations have some sort of statement on abortion (including several that are pro-choice), I would wager that most people in the pews are not aware of these statements and resolutions.

All of this is to say that, as on many other issues, including women's ordination or LGBTQ inclusion, Christians are divided on the issue of abortion. But I believe that we are not as divided as we think or as divided as the media would like to portray us. Finding common ground in the principles of our faith and who we believe God to be leads us to more complete and expansive "pro-life" principles that support the flourishing of all people.

CHRISTIANITY AND THE CULTURE WARS

Every day when we open a newspaper, watch the news on television, or scroll through our social media feeds, we encounter voices bemoaning the state of our nation. Those holding more traditional or conservative values view many of the social and legal changes in our country since the 1960s—the legality of abortion; the civil rights progress made by people of color and lesbian, gay, bisexual, and transgender individuals; the removal of prayer from public schools—as evidence of the decline. Those with more progressive or liberal values are similarly concerned, from the perspective that change has not gone far enough to protect minorities and vulnerable citizens or that the positive changes that have been made are at risk of being reversed.

These culture wars have, in part, been characterized by a particular type of Christianity that manifests itself in the public sphere. Rather than seeking unity, Christians on the right and the left, driven by fear and anxiety, are sucked into an ever-louder public discourse. Since the late 1970s, the religious right, made up of predominantly white, evangelical Protestants and conservative Catholics, has championed socially conservative political positions in line with the Republican Party. With their positions on issues like school prayer, contraception, and abortion rights, the Republican Party has often catered to conservative Christian groups like Focus on the Family and the Family Research Council.

Meanwhile, progressive Christians and those in mainline denominations have not had the same amount of political or cultural influence and often have been written out of the narrative altogether. The so-called religious left lacks a centralizing political organization and includes a diversity of viewpoints, which minimizes their impact on the political process, despite their politics being strongly influenced by their faith. The predominant social discourse and media reporting often equate "Christian" with those who make up the religious right and fail to acknowledge the nuance and diversity of opinions among those who call themselves followers of Christ.

In the United States of America, decades of these culture wars have divided people of faith so that instead of working together as the body of Christ, we are shouting at each other across a great divide. At times, it can even seem as if we are speaking different languages, with those of us in mainline denominations drawing from historical creeds, theologians, and science in addition to Scripture, while our evangelical family members insist that Scripture stands alone and must be interpreted literally.

Paul's letters to the Corinthians show us that divisions have existed between Christians since the early church; yet we also pray and work for a day when Jesus' prayer for his church might come true, that we all may be one (John 17:21). While we may never see eye to eye on certain issues, we may be surprised at what we can accomplish when we seek out and find common ground with those with whom we assume we disagree. Ultimately, we must believe that there is more that unites us than divides us, that despite holding a variety of opinions on certain cultural issues, we are all "called to the one hope of our calling, one Lord, one faith, one baptism" (Eph. 4:4–5).

ABORTION AND CHRISTIANITY

For Christians, the culture war battles around abortion and contraceptive rights are driven in large part by the theology of personhood. Since 1974, every year in January, anti-abortion activists flock to Washington, D.C., for the March for Life, to protest around the anniversary of the Supreme Court's decision in *Roe v. Wade*, as the March for Life website puts it, "to share the truth concerning the greatest human rights violation of our time, legalized abortion on demand." Politicians in conservative-leaning states appeal to their conservative Christian constituencies by proposing amendments to state constitutions and regulations on abortion clinics and by threatening to withhold federal funding from Planned Parenthood clinics. The goal of the religious right is that the Supreme Court ultimately overturn *Roe v. Wade* and return the issue to state governments, with the hope of making abortion illegal once again.

Christians who are in favor of legal access to safe abortions are rarely pro-abortion and do not consider the termination of a pregnancy a decision to be entered into lightly. Rather, they view the decision of whether to carry an unplanned pregnancy to term as a decision to be made by the woman, her medical team, her family, and others who might provide spiritual or personal counsel, rather than by a mandate from the government. They recognize that these decisions are not made in a vacuum, and that wealth inequality and racism are factors in health care. Decreased access to abortion and contraceptive services is more likely to affect women in poverty and women of color, making them less able to effectively plan their families, particularly in conservative, rural areas of the country, and thereby perpetuating cycles of poverty.

The term "pro-life" for anti-abortion activists deserves criticism when their positions on other life-giving issues suggest they may be more pro-birth than pro-life. When those who call themselves pro-life are also in favor of capital punishment and work to cut funding for programs that assist people with food, housing, and access to health care, they cannot be considered to have a consistent pro-life ethic. As Sister Joan Chittister, a Catholic nun, has said,

> I do not believe that just because you're opposed to abortion, that that makes you pro-life. In fact, I think in many cases, your morality is deeply lacking if all you want is a child born but not a child fed, not a child educated, not a child housed. And why would I think that you don't? Because you don't want any tax money to go there. That's not pro-life. That's pro-birth. We need a much broader conversation on what the morality of pro-life is.[1]

To standardize mass communications for American journalists, the Associated Press Stylebook instructs writers to use "anti-abortion" instead of "pro-life," and "pro-abortion rights" rather than "pro-choice"; but given the complexity and limitations of these terms, I will use all of these terms throughout the book as appropriate.

Outside of the usage of "pro-life" in the context of the discussion on abortion, I believe that Christians of all political stripes can find common ground in a commitment to being expansively pro-life, even as we might differ in how that is politically executed in our common life. Throughout Scripture, God reveals God's self to be pro-life, pro–human flourishing. God creates life out of dust. God rescues God's people from slavery and other anti-life conditions. God becomes incarnate in Jesus Christ, to live out God's pro-life mission through Jesus' ministry of healing and feeding and restoring people to community. Ultimately, through the death and resurrection of Jesus Christ, God defeats death once and for all, offering new life to all of humanity. Jesus says about his sheep, "I came that they may have life, and have it abundantly" (John 10:10).

I believe Christians can agree that the broken and sinful world we currently inhabit and the world that God desires for us are far apart, and that we share a longing for the coming of God's kingdom, a kingdom that is broadly pro-life and pro–human flourishing. We can pray and work for a world that is closer to what God intends for God's creation, where every child conceived is desired and every pregnancy is met with joy, where every birthed child is loved and cared for and raised in a household and a community that meet their physical, emotional, spiritual, and cultural needs. In an ideal world, the situations of rape, incest, and abuse that result in pregnancy would not exist, and the far too frequent choice between the health and survival of the mother and the termination of the pregnancy would never have to be made. Every sex act between two people would be one of mutual delight and joy and pleasure, an outpouring and bonding of love, never exploitative or a display of dominance.

However, our social and political realities demonstrate that we are far from this ideal world. There are concerns like the Zika virus spreading through Latin America, causing devastating birth defects for pregnant women and their children. In many Zika-affected countries abortion rights and access to affordable contraception are nonexistent or limited, leading health officials to ask women of childbearing age to refrain from getting pregnant for two years. Even though it takes two people to create a child, women are being asked to bear sole responsibility for their fertility with limited resources, or else suffer the consequences of a disabled child with special needs to whom she may not be able to offer adequate care. This is just one scenario that demonstrates the need for access to safe and legal contraception for all women, including procedures for terminating pregnancies.

COMPLICATING THE DIALOGUE

While I have supported a woman's right to bodily autonomy and to make medical decisions that are right for her and her family for a long time, the issues and questions raised by the rhetoric around abortion rights took on new meaning and significance as my friends and I moved into a life stage marked by marriage and children. Friends and family members suffered challenging pregnancies, miscarriages, and infertility, despite deeply desiring to have children. Other friends, taking seriously into account their life circumstances and support systems, made the decision to end unplanned pregnancies.

As I grieved with and supported these loved ones in their varying circumstances and challenges around reproduction, I realized that, scientifically, we were talking about the same biological entity. For families experiencing miscarriages, these groups of cells were a person, their child, for whom they had hopes and dreams and plans, even in the earliest stages of existence. This pregnancy was a joy, a happy occasion, and to lose it was devastating. For others choosing to terminate their pregnancies, this collection of cells was not yet a distinct human and certainly not compatible with life outside of the womb. Their pregnancies were unwelcome and stressful, and to terminate them was a relief.

Advances in medical technology allow us not only to hear a fetal heartbeat at week six of a pregnancy but also to diagnose possible issues and even perform surgery on a child in utero. Just a few decades ago, children born as early as thirty weeks would not have survived, but today, the care of neonatal intensive-care units can often help these premature babies continue to develop, survive, and thrive outside of the womb. These technologies are undeniably a good, though the inundation of information and testing adds another dimension and complication to conception, pregnancy, and childbirth.

Every pregnancy, every situation is unique, because it involves people, and people are complicated individuals with their own joys, griefs, and relationships. Sometimes people do horrible things to one another, as in the cases of rape and incest. Sometimes a woman's age or medical conditions make pregnancies difficult or dangerous. Sometimes contraception doesn't work the way it is supposed to; a woman accidentally skips a pill, a condom breaks, a vasectomy fails. Sometimes a family already has more children than they can support financially and emotionally. Conception and pregnancy are not always welcomed with joy and gratitude, even for a married couple.

In the movie *Waitress*, Keri Russell's character Jenna has been preparing to leave her no-good husband when she finds out that she is pregnant. When her doctor congratulates her on the pregnancy, she specifies in no uncertain terms that she is not happy about it, but she is planning on keeping the baby. The societal pressure for women to become mothers and graciously to welcome the sacrifices that entails is very strong.

Based on the 2008 abortion rate, the Guttmacher Institute concluded that one in three women will have an abortion by the age of forty-five. While the incidence of abortion may have declined since then, thanks in part to lower rates of teen pregnancies and better methods of birth control, this statistic illustrates how common abortion is. Perhaps even you, the reader, have had an abortion. The shame and stigma surrounding abortion and unwanted pregnancies, particularly in religious circles, are a huge impediment to having honest and forthright discussions about something nearly a third of women have gone through. I can only imagine that the shame and stigma of an unwanted pregnancy prevent many women from discussing these issues with a clergyperson or other spiritual mentor, given the vitriol with which the most vocal segments of Christianity discuss abortion.

If you are tired of the inflammatory and divisive rhetoric around abortion from the right and the left, this book is for you. If you are a Christian and ambivalent about abortion but don't want it to be outlawed, this book is for you. If you are looking for common ground with other Christians amid disagreement, this book is for you. If you believe that your faith has something to say about the lives of women and families, as well as unborn children, then this book is for you.

In the first two chapters, we will look at the political history of abortion and abortion laws in the United States to give us a sense of what abortion looked like before *Roe v. Wade* and how the political conversation has changed since then. In chapter 3, we will look at the impact that societal changes and medical technology have had on the debate concerning when life begins. Next, we will move on to what the Bible says about conception, birth, and life. Following that, we will look at what the church has had to say, how statements on abortion from denominational and church-wide bodies fit into this conversation. In chapter 6, we will work on reclaiming what it means to be pro-life and how that might support abortion access. Finally, we will finish with what we can do constructively to add to this ongoing conversation and discern steps to take action.

Chapter 1

A BRIEF HISTORY OF ABORTION FROM PREHISTORY TO ILLEGALITY

Since people have been having sex, men and women have invented ways to try to avoid the repercussions of sex, namely, pregnancy and sexually transmitted infections and diseases. Condoms, birth control, and induced abortions were not invented in the twentieth century, nor did people suddenly start having sex outside of marriage around the time of the sexual revolution in the 1960s. Overall, Christians and our institutional churches are not very good at talking about sex from a faith perspective, except to say, "Don't" or "Sex is for procreation, and that's it." Even if we agree that intimate physical relations find their deepest meaning within the commitment made in marriage, sex still serves purposes beyond and beside procreation, such as mutual pleasure, bonding, and expressing love and desire.

It is not clear how much ancient people understood about reproduction or the efficacy of their contraceptive methods. Prolonged breast-feeding was one means of delaying pregnancy, and ancient women undertook rituals and ingested herbs or simply avoided sexual intercourse at certain times during their menstrual cycles—what some today call the rhythm method. The ancient Egyptians and Chinese recorded contraception and abortion recipes that date back to 1300 BCE. Many of these recipes for contraception involved inserting something into the vagina that successfully killed and repelled sperm. Men used primitive condoms made of linen or animal intestine or would coat the penis with substances like tar to function as a barrier. Similar contraceptive methods are documented in the late ninth and early tenth centuries in Persia, where Islamic physicians considered contraception to be part of good medical care.

As shocking as it is to our modern sensibilities, one of the primary methods for limiting fertility and population growth in the ancient world was infanticide, or killing children after they were born.[1] Abortion methods were primarily nonsurgical and often ineffective or dangerous. Women engaged in strenuous activity, fasting, bloodletting, and massage to eliminate an unwanted pregnancy. By the Roman era, certain herbs were used as abortifacients, though this was not without risk to the woman, as many of those herbs were poisonous.

ABORTION AND THE EARLY CHURCH

Aristotle's teaching on "delayed ensoulment" was prominent in the world into which Christianity was born. The Greek philosopher held that the fetus first had a vegetable soul, which evolved later in pregnancy into an animal soul, and finally into a human soul. This "ensoulment" happened around forty days after conception for male fetuses and ninety days after conception for female fetuses. Without a means of determining the date of conception, or of knowing gender prior to birth, these numbers were mostly symbolic. Nonetheless, the concept of delayed ensoulment, which influenced Christian thinkers like Thomas Aquinas, suggests that, as the fetus develops, its moral standing as a person increases.

The Christian church began in a world in which widespread contraception, abortion, and infanticide were practiced by Egyptians, Jews, Greeks, and Romans; not surprisingly, the early thinkers in the church felt compelled to address these issues. When the early church fathers wrote about abortion, it was not ambiguous: abortion was considered murder. Both the second-century *Epistle of Barnabas* and the *Didache* contain commands not to murder a child by abortion or to commit infanticide. Tertullian, writing from North Africa in the third century, says,

> The embryo therefore becomes a human being in the womb from the moment that its form is completed. The law of Moses, indeed, punishes with due penalties the man who shall cause abortion, inasmuch as there exists already the rudiment of a human being, which has imputed to it even now the condition of life and death, since it is already liable to the issues of both, although, by living still in the mother, it for the most part shares its own state with the mother.[2]

In the fourth century, Gregory of Nyssa argues in a polemic against Christians who do not believe in the divinity of the Holy Spirit that an unborn child possesses a soul as far as it exhibits movement and growth, the soul being present in the unformed embryo and later made manifest, essentially arguing for ensoulment at conception.

We reach the heart of the issue in Clement of Alexandria's *The Tutor*, wherein he writes,

> But men are not always willing to let marriage serve its purpose. For marriage is the desire for the procreation of children, and not disorderly sexual conduct,

which is as much outside the laws as it is foreign to reason. Universal life would proceed according to nature if we would practice continence from the beginning instead of destroying, through immoral and pernicious acts, human beings who are given birth by Divine Providence. Those who use abortifacient medicines to hide their fornication are causing the outright destruction, together with the fetus, of the whole human race.[3]

Put simply, sex is only acceptable within marriage, and marriage is for the procreation of children.

A closer look at the beliefs of the early church fathers about the status of the fetus and abortion complicates matters. Considering the resurrection of the dead at the end of the world, Augustine concludes that early miscarried fetuses would not be included. Thus, for Augustine, it follows that at least the early fetus does not have the same status of person. Recently, Latin American theologians reached the conclusion that the texts condemning abortion in the early church refer to the abortion of a fully formed fetus, so the abortion of the early fetus would not rise to the level of murder.[4]

The condemnations of abortion and contraception in the early church can be read as a pro-life statement about the moral status of the fetus and also with a general bias against sex, sexuality, and women. Until the role of the ovum was discovered in the nineteenth century, sperm were thought to contain miniature people, or *homunculi*, which is why male masturbation was sometimes called homicide.[5] In addition to the fact that early Christians were ignorant of women's full role in reproduction, the history of Christianity is oftentimes virulently antiwomen, and these debates about sexuality and reproduction frequently reflect that. From blaming Eve for the fall of humanity to the Mosaic law assuming male ownership of women, women were sources of evil at worst and pieces of property at best.

Despite women being the last remaining disciples of Jesus at the foot of the cross and the first to witness and preach the resurrection, the legacy of women in the growing Christian movement was mostly erased. First-century Judaism was heavily patriarchal, and out of this milieu came the church. For a little while, it seemed that the church might buck the trends of the culture, as women led house churches and served as deaconesses. Many of the early church martyrs were women, and the church created a place for widows and others who might not have had a male family member to support and care for them. Even still, women were primarily viewed as property—to be transferred from father to husband when the time was right.

As many of us know well, Paul's letters have frequently been quoted in defense of complementarianism, the idea that men and women have "separate but equal" gifts. Women should not teach men and should be submissive to their husbands. However, Paul's letters also name the many women who were active leaders in these Christian communities, women like Lydia and Dorcas. And, of course, Paul boldly claims in Galatians 3:28 that in Christ Jesus there is neither Jew nor Greek, neither male nor female, neither slave nor free.

In the earliest days of the church, Christians saw one another as family, as brothers and sisters in Christ, a bond that trumped blood relations. They were encouraged to grow the church through evangelism and baptism, rather than through giving birth. After all, the kingdom was nigh, and Jesus would be returning soon, within a generation.

In his first letter to the church at Corinth, Paul writes that it is better for the unmarried and the widows to stay that way, unless they are unable to control themselves sexually (1 Cor. 7:9). He also recommends that those who are married remain so, but that "the time has been shortened" and "the form of this world is passing away" (1 Cor. 7:31). Two thousand years later, we're all still waiting for the second coming, and the Christian view of family has changed quite a bit.

The legacy of the early church fathers on the status and place of women is not a great one. Augustine wrote about women and reproduction, "I fail to see what use woman can be to man, if one excludes the function of bearing children."[6] Augustine also wrote that a woman alone does not possess the image of God, but does so only when taken together with a man. Tertullian writes, "Woman is a temple built over a sewer," and, referencing Eve, declares that women are the gate to hell. Another prevalent idea was that women are simply defective or misbegotten men. Thomas Aquinas thought that females are produced from male embryos that were damaged in the womb.[7]

Both inside and outside Christianity, women were frequently reduced to their ability to bear children, with language that still echoes in today's debates. From ancient Greece to Egyptian writings to the Qur'an, women are talked about as passive, as mere hosts for a prospective child. The man plants the seed in the soil, where it then grows. Despite the dangers of childbirth, "her effort, her needs, the dangers and pains and injuries of pregnancy and childbirth are all erased," says feminist writer Katha Pollitt.[8]

Until 1869, there was no official position within the Catholic Church about the status of the embryo and fetus. According to theologian Christine Gudorf,

The dominant, but not the only *theological* position was adopted from Aristotle and championed by Thomas Aquinas, who counted ensoulment of the fetus as occurring 40–80 days after conception, depending on the sex of the fetus. The dominant *pastoral* position—obviously because it was more practical and obvious—was that ensoulment occurred at quickening, when the fetus could first be felt moving in the mother's womb, usually early the fifth month. Before ensoulment the fetus was not understood as a person.[9]

Even in the early church, most Catholic thinkers denied the idea of "spontaneous animation," that life begins at conception. While abortion, along with sterilization, contraception, and masturbation, was considered a sin, it did not rise to the level of murder.

Despite the church's position on abortion and church canons that decreed punishments for women guilty of abortion, it appears that women still sought out abortions. Initially, as a penance for her abortion, a woman was excluded from communion for the rest of her life. Later, in the fourth century, this lifetime ban was shortened to a period of ten years, when she could be readmitted to communion if she was found to show sufficient repentance. While these penalties seem harsh, the church saw itself as trying to protect women, who frequently died from ingesting poison designed for abortion.

As the Roman Catholic Church came to dominate much of Europe through the Middle Ages, it limited reproductive practices and counseled celibacy for unmarried laypeople and sexual restraint within marriage; so contraceptive and abortive treatments went underground.

Though knowledge about the body and medical expertise increased during the Renaissance, women's health needs were met primarily by midwives rather than physicians. Unlike physicians, who trained at universities, midwives were typically older women who learned through apprenticing experience how to deliver babies and attend to women's reproductive health, including recipes for contraception and abortion. Later, women with this kind of knowledge were often accused of sorcery and witchcraft.

It is hard to imagine the plight and status of these premodern women, particularly since their voices and struggles were not preserved by history. With regard to sex, they were at the mercy of their husbands and without easy access to contraception. Premodern times saw frequent pregnancies, the very real possibility of dying in childbirth, and a high child mortality rate. Though the church fathers name only adultery and drunkenness as a reason for a woman to seek out an abortionist, we can imagine multiple reasons why a woman might feel the need to eliminate an unwanted pregnancy.

With the Protestant Reformation and the end of clerical celibacy, clergy began to have firsthand experience of the dilemmas of reproduction in the context of family life. Unsurprisingly, at the start, Protestantism was not resistant to family planning, and birth rates illustrate that Protestants were managing their fertility.[10] Nonetheless, early Protestant leaders who discussed abortion were firmly against it. In a commentary on Exodus 21:22, John Calvin writes, "For the fetus, though enclosed in the womb of its mother, is already a human being, and it is a monstrous crime to rob it of the life which it has not yet begun to enjoy. If it seems more horrible to kill a man in his own house than in a field, because a man's house is his place of most secure refuge, it ought surely to be deemed more atrocious to destroy a fetus in the womb before it has come to light."[11] Though opposed to abortion, Protestants lacked an "explicit moral reasoning" on why it was evil.[12]

ABORTION IN AMERICA

Puritans arriving in America wanted to grow their communities through reproduction based on the biblical directive to "be fruitful and multiply" and the need for assistance with farming and survival. The high rate of infant mortality contributed to frequent pregnancies, with the hope that at least a few children would survive to adulthood, but many women died in childbirth or faced serious gynecological problems. European techniques for controlling fertility also traveled to the New World in family Bibles, letters, and cookbooks; additionally, American Indians and slaves from Africa and the Caribbean taught white women about indigenous herbs that induced abortions.

Without ultrasounds, fetal monitors, and the other technologies that we take for granted today, women relied on feedback from their own bodies and from a community of women. During the colonial era and the early nineteenth century, women mistook early pregnancy for an obstruction of menses, which upset the equilibrium of the body and required the restoration of menstrual flow to bring the body back into balance.[13] This view was consistent with the medical theory at the time, which emphasized visible, sometimes violent measures, in order to restore the body to equilibrium when sickness upset it. Bleeding, blistering, and vomiting all pointed toward moving the body back to health and equilibrium. Thus women whose menses were blocked took drugs, often administered domestically with local herbs, and viewed the ensuing vomiting and evacua-tion as a positive sign that their menses would be restored.

At the end of the eighteenth century, with the upheaval of the American Revolution and similar revolutions around the world, women no longer saw themselves as inferior to men and pushed for equality, leading to decreased fertility and family size. Even during the Victorian era, when social standards for white upper- and middle-class women com-pelled women to devote themselves to home and family, advertisements for condoms, contraceptive devices, and preparations to induce abortion appeared in newspapers and periodicals in the 1860s. The situation was different for women of color. During slavery, female slaves were sub-ject to the rules of their owners, who often forbid slaves to terminate pregnancies, as those children would then belong to the slave owners and be sold, separating families. Free black women were more likely to work outside the home than their white counterparts but may not have had the same kind of access to contraceptives or abortion, due to a lack of education and financial resources.

With the industrial revolution and the urbanization of America, the need for lots of children to work on the family farm disappeared for many Americans. People living in cities had more facile access to knowledge, including lit-erature on reproductive issues. Public lectures, pamphlets, and books provided information about sexual anatomy, reproduction, the rhythm method (abstaining from sex during parts of a woman's menstrual cycle), and douching with spermicide. During this time, New York City sup-ported the business of more than two hundred abortionists, with varying degrees of competence and expertise.[14]

Suddenly male physicians with formal medical train-ing found themselves in competition with irregular medical practitioners like midwives and abortionists, who were overwhelmingly female. So in 1847 physicians formed the American Medical Association (AMA). By requiring a medical license to practice, the AMA put the irregular doctors out of business and subsequently took a strict antiabortion stance.

In addition to protecting their profession, there were racial motivations for their position on abortion. Physicians perceived that as more middle- and upper-class white women successfully limited the size of their families, the proportion of the white population in America would decline, and they were afraid that free blacks and immigrants entering the country would outpace the more desirable American-born white population. Dr. Horatio R. Storer led the medical campaign against abortion, erasing the distinction between earlier and later stages of pregnancy and equating it with infanticide.

Prior to Dr. Storer's campaign, the common-law understanding around fetal development prioritized "quickening," when a woman would first feel movement in her womb, sometime around the midpoint of pregnancy. It was at this point that a pregnancy became really real and necessitated carrying it to term. As Leslie Reagan describes it, this sensation "had emotional, social, and legal meaning," but in the nineteenth century it was denigrated by antiabortion doctors as unreliable.[15] In targeting "quickening," doctors claimed for themselves the territory of pregnancy, snatching it away from women's own experiences and delegitimizing a woman's perception of her own pregnancy. As medicine became professionalized (predominantly by men), women were no longer seen as the foremost experts on their own bodies. The midwives, doulas, and herbalists who had served women for millennia were replaced by formally educated physicians who sought to position themselves as the ultimate experts.

The challenges of a more modern and secularized society were not confined to the United States. In 1869, Pope Pius IX issued the document *Apostolicae Sedis Moderationi*, which, among other things, eliminated the distinction between an "inanimate" and an "animate" fetus, declaring that abortion at any stage of pregnancy was equivalent to murder. The subsequent penalty for abortion at any stage was excommunication from the church; this laid the groundwork for future canon law that ruled abortion morally unacceptable in every circumstance, as the fetus was "ensouled" at conception.

In the 1870s, Anthony Comstock arrived in New York City from Connecticut and was shocked by the immorality he perceived. Prostitutes were openly advertised, young men had access to pornographic pictures and magazines, and drugstore shelves publicly displayed contraceptive devices. A federal law passed in 1865 outlawed any "obscene book, pamphlet, picture, print, or other publication . . . [of] vulgar and indecent character" sent through the mail, but it did not include advertisements.[16] As the head of the New York Society for the Suppression of Vice (NYSSV), Comstock effectively lobbied the federal government for an amendment. In 1873, Congress officially passed the Act for the Suppression of Trade in and Circulation of Obscene Literature and Articles of Immoral Use, colloquially the Comstock Act. It restricted obscene or lewd materials sent through the mail, and for the first time, the prohibited items included "any article or thing designed or intended for the prevention of conception or procuring of abortion."[17] Twenty-four states proceeded to pass similar laws, with some even penalizing private discussions about contraception or abortion. In 1879 Connecticut outlawed the use of contraceptive devices and medicines entirely.

In reality, things changed slowly in the reproductive lives of most women and even the practice of physicians, as abortion was still widely accepted and carried out. Birth control devices and abortifacients were available on the black market and spoken about in code. Although outlawing abortion was initially intended to encourage white upper- and middle-class women to grow their families, these women often had fewer problems finding and paying for what they needed, dividing society between those who could afford contraception and abortion and those who could not. These laws also silenced public discussion about sexual intimacy, contraception, and abortion.

Chapter 2

BEFORE AND AFTER
ROE V. WADE

In the end, abortion was illegal in the United States for approximately one hundred years, from the Comstock Act in 1873 to *Roe v. Wade* in 1973. Particularly in the late nineteenth century and first half of the twentieth century, women desperately sought out reproductive care that met their needs, which was often illegal and unprofessional. Margaret Sanger's experience as a nurse delivering the babies of poor working-class women in New York City in the early twentieth century compelled her openly to defy the Comstock Act. As she described it, "[p]regnancy was a chronic condition among the women of this class."[1] First, she authored informative columns about sex, pregnancy, and abortion in a socialist newspaper called the *New York Call*; when she was prosecuted under the Comstock Act, she fled the country.

After her return, along with her sister, Ethel Byrne, she opened an illegal birth-control clinic in 1916 in Brooklyn. They were both arrested and sentenced to time in jail. Sanger successfully appealed her case and fought for women to obtain contraceptives legally in order to prevent dangerous pregnancies. In 1921 she established the American Birth Control League (ABCL), which opened clinics offering reproductive health services in larger cities around the country.

Opposition to contraception, at least for Catholics, was linked to opposition to abortion, and these two were similarly linked in the Comstock Laws. Catholics viewed contraception as an affront to natural law, a position that Pope Pius XI took in his anticontraceptive encyclical *Casti Connubii* in 1930. Contraception separated sex from procreation, challenged God's authority as the Creator by attempting to sabotage the formation of new human life, and treated human life as something to be prevented rather than valued.[2]

Thousands of women benefited from increased access to birth control in the 1920s, but contraception during this era also had its dark side: eugenics. Sanger and some of her allies endorsed the use of birth control to limit the reproductive capabilities of poor, sexually promiscuous, or mentally disabled women, particularly if they were African American. While hoping that poor women would voluntarily reduce their birth rates by using contraception, more coercive means were certainly used. Under legal programs of sterilization of criminals or the mentally disabled, which were upheld by the Supreme Court, sixty thousand Americans were sterilized against their wills.[3] For Catholics, voluntary contraception and eugenics programs were two sides of the same coin—a fundamental disrespect for the divine gift of human life.

Protestants shared with Catholics a sense of the value of fetal life and a concern about sex outside of marriage, which they believed was promoted by the availability of abortion and contraception.[4] Due to the influence of Margaret Sanger, however, middle-class Protestants came to embrace contraceptive devices, and by the late 1930s many Protestant church bodies had officially endorsed birth control. Protestants who endorsed birth control still declared their opposition to abortion, and, like Sanger, saw contraception as an antiabortion measure. For Catholics, it was a very short step from contraception to abortion, while Protestants saw no link between the two. The difference between Protestant and Catholic views on birth control and the divide to which it led cannot be underestimated.

THE GROWING CALLS FOR REPEAL

The first widespread calls for legalized abortion were issued in the 1930s, less than half a century after abortion had been prohibited in most states. When the Great Depression hit at the tail end of the 1920s, families had economic reasons for reliable contraception to keep their families small: millions of workers had lost their jobs. Desperation and anxiety led to nearly one million abortions yearly during the early 1930s.[5] During this time, abortion became more available and visible and moved from private offices and homes to hospitals and clinics. Courts began to overturn Comstock laws, as the Depression helped to legitimate contraceptives.

Poor women and black women were still more likely to self-induce abortions, and consequently they suffered more complications, entering the hospital for care.[6] Women suffering from septic abortions or other obstetrical infections postabortion caused doctors and public health reformers to realize the link between illegal abortion and maternal mortality, and a few physicians began to talk and write publicly in favor of loosening or even repealing abortion laws. Some physicians sought to provide women with a safe and legal way to terminate pregnancies in hospitals. Nonetheless, these doctors were anything but "pro-abortion"; rather, they saw legalization as the lesser of two evils. William J. Robinson, a leading advocate of birth control and a self-identified humanist, wrote that abortion "does mean the destruction of a commencing life" and hoped that access to contraceptives would make it a rare occurrence.[7]

During and after World War II, societal structures shifted again. While many women worked during the war years, the postwar baby boom promoted the ideal of a woman who married, had babies, and stayed home to take care of her family. Women continued to seek abortions for unwanted pregnancies, and legal therapeutic abortions were available in the case of threat to emotional or physical health, evidence of fetal abnormalities, or as a result of rape or incest, as long as women went before a hospital committee. Many hospital committees also mandated sterilization as a condition for therapeutic abortion, effectively punishing women for perceived irresponsible sexual behavior.

Through the 1950s, abortion laws gradually liberalized, in part to bring the law into alignment with medical practice and protect both women and the physicians who were providing abortions. Despite advances in medical technology in the twentieth century—penicillin and surgical techniques for Caesarean sections, for example—that decreased maternal mortality, women were still seeking abortions. In 1961, the American Law Institute suggested that abortion should be legal in cases of rape or incest, endangerment of a woman's physical or mental health, or suspected fetal deformity, so long as a two-doctor committee approved. The same year, the National Council of Churches passed a resolution condemning abortion in general but also explicitly allowing it in cases when a pregnancy endangered a woman's life or health.[8] Catholics, however, sought to limit the loopholes that allowed physicians in hospitals to provide therapeutic abortions, contributing to the continuing Catholic-Protestant division.

By the 1960s, the birth-control pill was on the market, and views about motherhood and careers began to change. The sexual revolution was in full swing, but many were threatened by the changes in traditional views on sex and sexuality, as well as by the demand by African Americans for civil rights and equality. At the same time, the Catholic Church was losing its political power in the wake of the Second Vatican Council. With the landmark Supreme Court case *Griswold v. Connecticut*, the court in 1965 ruled that a married couple could use contraceptives within the privacy of their relationship without interference by the government. While many individual states had reached this conclusion, this case made the decision at the federal level. The 1972 decision in *Eisenstadt v. Baird* extended that right to unmarried couples as well. Contraceptives were no longer treated as immoral and illegal by most Americans, and even many Catholics concluded that the use of birth control was an issue of personal morality rather than politics.[9]

On April 5, 1965, Walter Cronkite reported for *CBS Reports* on "Abortion and the Law," declaring that there was currently an "abortion epidemic" of up to one million abortions a year and a vast conflict between the law and a reality in which medical, social, and economic reasons for abortions were not recognized as valid. In interviews with those on both sides of the argument, the program portrayed the reality for many women of the time. Some women self-induced abortions and suffered hemorrhage or infection. Those with means traveled to Puerto Rico, Mexico, or overseas for legal abortions. Some abortion providers risked their own careers and reputations to provide women with safe procedures, while others used the opportunity to extort money from women and their partners. That a news program would devote an entire hour to covering this issue in a fair and balanced manner says a lot about the state of discourse around abortion in 1965. It is difficult to imagine a similar program today.

Despite disagreements, for most of the 1960s, people on both sides of the abortion debate generally agreed that the law should restrict abortion to some extent. The liberalization laws simply expanded the number of legitimate legal reasons for an abortion, and appeal to a hospital abortion committee was still necessary for approval. While the public desired greater freedom for doctors, they did not favor women choosing to terminate their pregnancies on demand.[10] In the mid-1960s a few activists began to push for the legalization of all abortions, using the language of feminism: a woman's right to her own body, and the right to an abortion as a part of women's freedom.

Between 1967 and 1973, several states began to reform and repeal the most restrictive abortion laws, legalizing therapeutic abortions and permitting abortions when a woman and her doctor viewed the procedure as necessary. A 1964 epidemic of rubella and birth defects among English babies whose mothers had taken the antinausea drug thalidomide led to the consideration of children's quality of life as another aspect of the conversation about reproduction. These conversations about fetal deformities also made Catholics nervous as they recalled eugenics arguments from earlier in the century.

During this time, several pro-life groups successfully linked a comprehensive ethic of life—including social justice and an anti-war stance—to fight against abortion legalization at the state level. Initially a primarily Catholic effort, groups like the Minnesota Citizens Concerned for Life (MCCL) also attracted Protestants, advocates of contraception, and members of Planned Parenthood with their politically progressive ethos. While the short-term goal was to stop abortion liberalization bills in the state legislature, their ultimate goal was "to create a society in which women did not feel the need to resort to abortions" by providing counseling and medical and financial assistance.[11] Against the backdrop of the Vietnam War, a growing minority of young, politically progressive pro-lifers, particularly on college campuses, campaigned against violence in all forms, from abortion to war, capital punishment, economic injustice, and environmental issues. Groups like Save Our Unwanted Life (SOUL) and the National Youth Pro-Life Coalition (NYPLC) that advocated for a comprehensive pro-life ethic were eventually marginalized within the right-to-life movement as the cause drew more politically conservative evangelical Christians and ultimately became polarized along partisan lines.

In 1970 lawyers Sarah Weddington and Linda Coffee joined forces to represent Norma McCorvey, known as Jane Roe, in order to challenge the abortion statute in Texas. *Roe v. Wade* was argued in front of the Supreme Court in December 1971 and October 1972, and on January 22, 1973, the court issued its decision, which had national significance. The Fourteenth Amendment's guarantee of the right to privacy, which undergirded previous decisions like *Griswold* and *Eisenstadt*, was found to be "broad enough to encompass a woman's decision whether or not to terminate her pregnancy." The court ruled that a woman's right to an abortion during the first trimester was absolute, but they also left the door open for other regulations and restrictions by state governments.

Weddington wrote later, "The Court's decision was an opportunity for all women. The battle was never 'for abortion'—abortion was not what we wanted to encourage. The battle was for the basic right of women to make their own decisions. There was a basic question underlying the specific issue of abortion: Who is to control and define the lives of women? And our answer was: Not the government!"[12]

It is worth noting that five of the seven Supreme Court justices in the majority opinion of *Roe v. Wade* were appointed by Republican presidents, so it was hardly a superliberal court. Justice Harry Blackmun felt that the decision was a measured compromise, though it required that forty-six states liberalize their abortion laws and explicitly deprived the fetus of personhood and constitutional protection. As Blackmun said, "The Court does not today hold that the Constitution compels abortion on demand."[13] Rather than passively accepting the decision, antiabortion advocates geared up for a continued fight, focused on overturning the decision of the Supreme Court.

AFTER *ROE V. WADE*

In the decades since that landmark Supreme Court decision, open access to legal and safe abortion has brought about benefits to women, particularly low-income women and women of color, who had previously had the least access to skilled practitioners and were most likely to be injured or die as a result of illegal abortion. Legalized abortion had an impact on public health, as maternal mortality rates dropped dramatically. As Katha Pollitt writes in her book *Pro: Reclaiming Abortion Rights*,

Legalizing abortion didn't just save women from death and injury and fear of arrest. . . . It changed how women saw themselves: as mothers by choice, not fate. As long as abortion is available to her, even a woman who thinks it is tantamount to murder is making a choice when she keeps a pregnancy. . . . *Roe v. Wade* gave women a kind of existential freedom that is not always welcome—indeed, is sometimes quite painful—but that has become part of what women are.[14]

However, *Roe v. Wade* stood in stark opposition to popular opinion, which was very nearly evenly divided. Polls from the 1970s show that approximately half of the public opposed elective abortion, and four out of ten people believed it to be murder.[15] Catholics (and Protestants distressed by changing sexual mores) suddenly found themselves shocked by a country that seemed to go against the very laws of God. Whereas the Supreme Court was the guarantor of civil rights in the 1960s, some now saw it as an enemy of the fundamental human right to life.

Antiabortion activists have been successful at limiting access to abortion in some states and changing the tenor of the conversation. While earlier pro-life coalitions were politically diverse, after the late 1970s, the pro-life movement largely abandoned the more politically and socially progressive vision. The first blow to *Roe v. Wade* came in 1976 with the passage of the Hyde Amendment, sponsored by Illinois congressman Henry Hyde, which banned Medicaid funding for abortions for low-income women, a law that was later upheld by the Supreme Court. By 1980, the Republican Party platform included "a constitutional amendment to restore protection of the right to life for unborn children," and religious activists became vocal about their belief that life begins at conception.[16] Politicians have unsuccessfully sought constitutional amendments at the state and federal level like the Human Life Amendment or Fetal Personhood Amendments, which would guarantee the right to life from the moment of conception.

The Supreme Court ruling in *Planned Parenthood v. Casey* in 1992, in which states could enact laws restricting abortion before viability for purposes other than protecting a woman's health, led to another wave of legislation in state and local legislatures around the country. These laws often include preabortion counseling, waiting periods, and requiring parental consent for an abortion for a minor. In 2007, the Supreme Court permitted an abortion restriction without an exception for a mother's health, the so-called Partial Birth Abortion Act, which prohibits a procedure that is already rare and dictates how doctors can practice medicine.

More recent legislative and legal challenges have centered on the Patient Protection and Affordable Care Act of 2010, known colloquially as Obamacare, as some businesses and religious institutions object to covering contraception under the insurance provided to their employees. Under the Religious Freedom Restoration Act, some states permit employers, hospitals, and organizations to refuse to cover contraception costs in their employee health-care plans for religious reasons. Some even permit pharmacists to refuse to provide any form of contraception, and a few permit pharmacies to refuse to provide emergency contraception.

The antiabortion movement has successfully pushed for state laws that restrict and even close abortion clinics via excessive regulation, known as Targeted Regulation of Abortion Provider (TRAP) laws. These require doctors performing abortions to have admitting privileges at nearby hospitals, require clinic hallways to be a certain size, and set other standards similar to those that surgery clinics must meet, even though the procedures occurring in surgery clinics are much more dangerous than abortion. Legislators say that these regulations make abortion, an already safe procedure, safer; in actuality, they are thinly veiled attempts to close clinics. Data from the Guttmacher Institute shows that the number of states with TRAP laws has more than doubled since the year 2000, and some states have few or no abortion providers.[17]

However, the June 2016 Supreme Court ruling in *Whole Women's Health v. Heller* favored abortion access. In a 5–3 decision, the Supreme Court overturned 2013 Texas law HB2, which imposed restrictions on abortion clinics, most notably requiring admitting privileges at nearby hospitals and meeting building specifications like those of ambulatory surgical centers. The specific targeting of women's health clinics was found to place an "undue burden" on women seeking an abortion. This ruling served as a warning to other state legislatures considering similar restrictions on abortion providers.

WHERE TO NEXT

A look at the history of abortion and in countries that now have very restrictive policies illustrates that banning or restricting abortion does not eliminate abortion; it either drives it underground or leads women to make dangerous choices. There is no way to eliminate abortion, but laws banning safe abortion have negative consequences for women and their families. As Leslie J. Reagan writes, "Making abortion hard to obtain will not return the United States to an imagined time of virginal brides and stable families; it will return us to the time of crowded septic abortion wards, avoidable deaths, and the routinization of punitive treatment of women by state authorities and their surrogates."[18] The concern of state surveillance of a woman's reproductive system no longer seems far-fetched. In Indiana, Puryi Patel was arrested and tried for feticide after suffering a miscarriage. Some states have laws criminalizing drug use by pregnant women. Not only do these laws privilege the fetus over the woman, but they also discourage appropriate prenatal care when women are afraid to seek out medical care for fear of arrest.

It seems as if every new legislative session brings measures intended to limit abortion in many conservative and "purple" states. Several states now have "twenty-week bans," despite 99 percent of abortions occurring before twenty-one weeks. Those that do take place later in pregnancy frequently involve wanted pregnancies and complex circumstances involving the mother and baby's health. At the same time, many so-called "pro-life" politicians do little to address measures that would support women and their families by providing adequate maternal health care, equal pay, a raise in the minimum wage, and mandatory paid family leave.

In Texas, a state that is notoriously hostile to abortion rights, the maternal mortality rate doubled over a two-year period, according to a report in the September 2016 issue of *Obstetrics and Gynecology*. Alarmingly, the authors wrote that the flood of deaths was hard to explain "in the absence of war, natural disaster, or severe economic upheaval." The increase in the maternal mortality rate coincides with slashing of the state's family planning budget, forcing more than eighty family-planning clinics around the state to close.[19] While conservative legislators seek to eliminate abortion, they do little to provide mothers with adequate health care.

As both political parties have become more polarized on abortion, they have failed to actually help women and children. Some Republican legislators propose bills that are blatantly unconstitutional and have little chance of passing in order to cater to their pro-life base. On the other side, Governor Andrew Cuomo of New York, an outspoken pro-choice Democrat, let a bill called the Women's Equity Act fail in 2013 because the legislature would not pass one of the provisions that expanded late-term abortion access. Rather than removing it and passing pay equity and a ban on pregnancy discrimination, Governor Cuomo let the bill fail. Both parties seem more concerned about virtue-signaling through their positions on abortion rather than passing legislation to help and support women and children, some which might even depress the abortion rate. With the increasing polarization of our political system, this seems unlikely to get better. Since *Roe v. Wade*, much in society has changed; women have entered the workforce, and intersectional movements for equality have become commonplace. Additionally, scientific advances have affected the ways in which we relate to our bodies and our sexuality. While some view the changes since the 1950s in a negative light, as the collapse of societal mores, others see them as living more fully into the constitutional promises of "life, liberty, and the pursuit of happiness" for all people.

Now we'll turn to the social and cultural milieu in which we find ourselves today.

Chapter 3

FAITH AND FERTILITY
IN A CHANGING CULTURE

As a young, married woman of childbearing age, I've spent a lot of time, energy, and money managing my fertility. While scientific and technological advances have made that safer and easier than ever, it is still something that I (along with my husband) deal with. Unlike other women, the privileges afforded to me by my race, class, education, and sexual orientation and identification make it easy for me to access the reproductive health care I need.

These days I can track my menstrual cycle on my smartphone by logging the quality of my cervical mucus, energy level, cramps, and sexual activity.[1] My phone predicts when I am ovulating and fertile, and when I will menstruate. Like most women, my cycle is not regular; it fluctuates, depending on travel, diet, stress, and exercise load. I've learned what my body tends to feel like during different points in my cycle. When I was taking a hormonal birth-control pill, my husband and I learned that I was likely to be particularly irritable and moody when I was taking the darkest blue pill, what we termed "blue week." Women know about the rhythms and cycles of their bodies, but often throughout history that knowledge has been discouraged or even considered witchcraft by religious authorities. Now that we've traced the political and legal history of abortion, let us situate abortion in today's context.

SOCIAL

As a young woman in the twenty-first century, I often take for granted the opportunities that are available to me. Looking at the scope of history, I see that it was not long ago at all that I would not have been able to pursue my calling to ordained Christian ministry. But when I was growing up, there was no question that I could do anything I put my mind to, regardless of gender—play sports, focus on science and math, study music and literature. My mother was a corporate lawyer, a competitive amateur athlete, and a mom with two kids—to me, the very definition of "having it all." Our economic status also allowed for a lot of help: nannies to chauffeur my brother and me to our after-school activities, a service to clean our house, take-out meals or prepared foods instead of cooking at home from scratch. Some of my friends' mothers did not work outside the home, but many others did. There were times when I wished that my mother was available to chaperone field trips and act as "classroom mom," like other moms.

In some ways, I believed that I grew up in a "postgender" society. I soaked in messages of female empowerment, that I too could have it all: a family and a satisfying career. Underlying this was an immense amount of privilege. First and foremost, I believed that I would be able to choose whether or not I worked outside the home. The economic situation of many women does not allow for this choice; it mandates that they have at least one full-time job to help provide for their families. With the onset of the Great Recession shortly after I graduated from college, many people were left unemployed or underemployed for years.

In my social milieu, educational and professional achievements were most important. Marriage and having children might come later, if at all. Both school and church told us to wait until marriage to have sex, and they underscored the importance of abstinence with statistics about teen pregnancy, sexually transmitted diseases, and purity culture. With marriage in the far distant future, abstinence seemed unlikely, but I also understood the purpose of waiting until I was more mature and in the right relationship. My faith and the lessons that I learned at church influenced my burgeoning sexual ethic. I understood that sexual intimacy was special and that my body and soul were intertwined, not separate.

Within my family, it was unspoken but understood that safe sex was of utmost importance, and, when I needed it, they would help me get contraception. Having children outside of marriage was definitely frowned upon, and while no one I knew personally growing up had an abortion (that I'm aware of), I heard rumors about other girls at my high school. In fact, the rumor in the hallways at my private school was that if you were visibly pregnant, you could no longer attend classes there.

When I got married at twenty-three, a year after graduating from college, I was the first of my peers to say "I do." While we were in love and had been dating for an acceptable amount of time, the logistics of medical residency and my place in the discernment process for ordination to the priesthood meant that living together long-term before marriage was not an option. Had we not had those external circumstances, I imagine we would have postponed marriage for a year or two.

It is hard to underestimate the vast cultural and social shifts around dating, marriage, and reproduction from previous generations to mine, shifts that have also affected the authority of the church. Among those from my parents' generation or older, it was not uncommon to get married very young. The stigma around singleness was in full effect, and one didn't dare show up pregnant out of wedlock. While some women of their social standing worked outside the home, it was clear that their primary duties were the care and feeding of spouse and children. Many of the older women in my congregation fawn over my husband for cleaning the dishes while I cook, though I see that as an expected, fair division of labor.

The change in perceptions of gender roles over the last fifty to sixty years has left its mark on marriage and family life. The women's liberation movement, the sexual revolution, and the increase of women's participation in the labor force changed how we think about the role and place of women. It is not only the stigmas around cohabitation and singleness that have changed, but also rates of divorce, which peaked at the oft-quoted 50 percent in the 1980s.

Some conservatives bemoan these changes, blaming feminism for the downfall of the American family and the general chaos in society. If women had only stayed in their place and been content with housework and the few occupations open to them, the building blocks of society would have remained strong and firm. While stability and safety in family life are crucial for raising children, just because two people are legally married does not mean those conditions exist. Abuse and addiction run through too many families, regardless of economic station and marital status. And while this might be a new dynamic for white families, women of color have been working outside the home for a while, usually in the role of caring for other people's homes and families.

Because I had grown up in such a supportive bubble, it was shocking to run into overt sexism, particularly in the church that I loved so much. During my discernment process, a bishop directly questioned how my husband and I were planning to raise kids with both of us having demanding vocations. At the time, we weren't even married yet. I received criticism about my voice while preaching, and I politely smiled every time I was told I was "too pretty to be a minister." Despite my feminist ideal of independence, I found myself financially reliant on my husband and forced into flexibility regarding my own vocational and professional opportunities.

In short, I have learned that there is no right way to be a woman. If you work outside the home, you are abandoning your children. If you stay at home, you are a traitor to feminism and the women who worked so hard to break those glass ceilings. If you wear makeup or shave your legs, you are a tool of the patriarchy. If you don't wear makeup, no one will take you seriously. A woman should be feminine but not too sexy, pretty but not distracting. If we aren't being paid equally or considered for promotions we deserve, we should "lean in," but we shouldn't be too aggressive or demanding. My friends who are parents report that motherhood is similar, as if there is an ideal that no one can ever live up to, but if we don't, then it is our own fault. Playing right into the hands of the patriarchy that seeks to limit our collective power, it is often women who engage in these criticisms of other women.

Some of the most virulent judgment falls on women for the size and shape of their families. Whether a woman has a child outside of marriage, chooses not to have children or is unable to have them, or decides to have many children, people have an opinion about it. There seems to be no end to the questions, starting on one's wedding day with "When are you going to start having children?"

A woman with a single child is asked, "Don't you want to have another?" A woman with two young girls is asked, "Aren't you thinking about trying for a boy?" A woman with five children is assumed to be very religious or odd, as people snidely comment under their breath, "Hasn't she heard of birth control?" Just a couple generations ago, it was not unheard of for people to have upward of ten children, the better to assist with farming tasks and to defend against high infant mortality rates. While the ideal size and shape of a family have changed through time and location, the current ideal seems to be a married man and woman with two children, one of each sex, as if people can just pick them off the shelves at the family store.

Today, thanks in part to the ruling in *Griswold v. Connecticut* in 1965 that reinforced marital privacy and allowed married couples legally to use birth control, we respect the right of each woman and her family to choose how big or small the family will be, even if we gossip about it. In the United States, no married couple is forced to procreate or to terminate a pregnancy; these are decisions made within the privacy of a family. Even within marriage, women have been managing their fertility as long as women have been having sex. Not that this has always been easy. Too many women have died in the past from pregnancies that were too close together or too dangerous—not to mention the risks inherent in childbirth. I consider myself fortunate to live when and where I do; the worst I have to deal with is nosy strangers and family members asking rude questions about the state of my uterus.

Even before widespread, effective contraceptive methods, women controlled the size of their families through contraception and abortion. How else do we explain the decline in the birth rate during the Great

Depression? As much as some people might like to believe it, people didn't just stop having sex. And yet that seems to be the response from people who are gravely uncomfortable with separating sex from reproduction. If you aren't ready to suffer the consequences of sex, keep your legs shut. These directives are also generally directed toward women, while men are free to do as they please, as if it did not take two people to make a baby.

This mentality is also less than helpful for married women who desire intimacy with their spouse but are not necessarily looking to grow their families. Even when women deliberately abstain from sex, the possibility of sexual violence can lead to an unwanted pregnancy. Based on the words of former Missouri congressman Todd Akin, that women's bodies can just "shut that whole thing down" in the event of a pregnancy from rape, it is clear that some of our elected officials don't understand basic biology.

A primary goal of feminism is to ensure that women have the freedom to make their own choices. Working outside the home or not, big or small families, marriage or not, women should make the choices that are right for them and that align with their faith and values. Today families take all kinds of shapes and sizes, with divorced and blended families more of a norm than an anomaly. The social stigma against out-of-wedlock births has decreased, and many parents have coparenting arrangements outside of marital bonds. There has also been a rise in grandparents becoming the primary caregivers for grandchildren. Instead of *Leave It to Beaver*, we have *Parenthood*, the early-twenty-first-century television drama that incorporated interracial relationships, parenting a child on the autism spectrum, health challenges, infidelity, and other issues that are part of family life.

Too often, pro-choice is interpreted as proabortion—rather than, well, pro-choice, in terms of all the choices that women make about how, when, and whether to bear and raise children. A pro-choice Christian ethic doesn't only mean supporting access to abortion services; it also means respecting and supporting the choice to have a child, even when a pregnancy was unplanned or unwanted. Pro-choice means respecting choices about contraception types and usage and working for women to have access to what works best for them and their lives. There is no "one size fits all" plan for every woman. Even if I personally cannot imagine choosing to terminate a pregnancy, my experience is only my experience; rather than condemning someone's choice, we are called by Christ to have empathy. Pro-choice Christians often highlight the fact that Jesus never shamed women, recalling the myriad encounters that Jesus has with women who are caught in some kind of sin. In John 8, Jesus rescues an adulterous woman from death by stoning and tells her, "Go and sin no more." Jesus neither affirms all of her decisions nor ridicules or shames her for them, but interacts with her as a capable, fully human being.

Too often the rest of the world stands in judgment of the choices women make, and that frequently includes the church as well. While our faith should influence and inform those choices, as Christians we should seek empathy and understanding before judgment.

MEDICAL

Our scientific and medical progress over the past fifty years has led to some complicated and challenging ethical issues with which people of faith have struggled. Research on embryonic stem cells and growing embryos in a lab bring up some of the same issues that abortion touches on—like the question of personhood. Is a fertilized egg really a person in the same way that you are a person or I am a person, not just a potential person? What characterizes "life"? Where once these questions fell within the purview of philosophers and theologians, now, with a lack of a common grounding in faith, we turn to science to help answer them.

No medical innovation changed the discussion around reproduction like the advent of oral contraceptives, or "the pill," a hormonal pill first approved by the Federal Drug Administration for contraception in 1960. Other medical contraceptives such as intrauterine devices, implants, vaginal rings, and injections, as well as the emergency contraceptive pill, popularly known as Plan B, followed over the next fifty years. While these developments have been game changers, there is still room for improvement. Many women suffer side effects from contraception, including mood swings and weight gain, and there remains no reversible method that is 100 percent effective in preventing pregnancy. Furthermore, despite barriers for many women in acquiring reliable contraceptives, the onus for preventing pregnancy is born almost solely by women. Outside of abstinence and withdrawal, male birth control is limited to condoms and vasectomies.

Today we know that semen does not contain a small man, that a fertilized egg requires both sexes and looks more like a blob of cells than a child. We know that it takes six to twelve days after fertilization to travel down the fallopian tube and attach to the uterine wall, at which point it is known as a blastocyst and has seventy to a hundred cells. Most women might not even be aware that they are pregnant for several weeks after a fertilized egg implants in the uterus, and about half of all fertilized eggs fail to implant at all and are expelled from the body during menstruation. Medical science maintains that pregnancy begins once the fertilized egg is implanted, as pregnancy is defined as the changes a woman's body undergoes to produce a baby.

The development of the ultrasound has also altered the abortion debate. The ability to view an embryo, even in a grainy black-and-white picture, seems to prove something beyond the changes that a woman experiences in her own body. The pictures of a developing fetus from an ultrasound have made the fetal personhood argument more persuasive to many people. More than an invisible, fluttering ball of cells, parents are able to see a small human beginning to take shape. Expectant parents sometimes share these images, not only on the refrigerator but on social media as well, to announce that their family is growing.

While the pro-life movement claims ultrasounds as a victory for their side, others downplay their significance. "Most of the 1 in 3 American women who will have had at least one abortion by menopause will have also seen a sonogram," Pollitt says, "given that 6 in 10 women who have abortions have already carried a pregnancy to term."[2] If anything, the use of ultrasound to diagnose fetal abnormalities may very well have led to more abortions for medical reasons.

Some states have passed laws that require women to undergo ultrasound scans or listen to the fetal heartbeat before abortion, with the idea that this will change a woman's mind by humanizing the fetus. The secondary purpose of these ultrasound laws—in some cases requiring that a doctor, instead of the usual hospital technician, perform the ultrasound—is to further complicate the abortion process and make it more expensive. Abortion opponents have claimed that 78–90 percent of women change their minds due to viewing a sonogram, but a 2014 study in *Obstetrics and Gynecology* found that of the 42.5 percent of abortion patients who voluntarily looked at the ultrasound, 98.4 percent stuck to their decision to end the pregnancy, and the 1.6 percent who changed their minds were already part of the 7.4 percent of patients who were ambivalent about the decision.[3]

Scientific and medical advances have also allowed genetic diseases and conditions to be diagnosed in utero. Various scans and tests can verify that the baby is healthy and developing well, or prepare a family in advance for a child with special needs. Far too often, these diagnoses force a family into a difficult choice, particularly if they do not have the resources to care for a special needs child, there is danger to the woman or the baby, or the baby is likely to die in the womb or shortly after birth.

These matters lead to uncomfortable questions about when abortion becomes eugenics, particularly in matters of nonfatal disabilities. Ninety percent of fetuses diagnosed with Down syndrome are aborted, despite the possibility for a high quality of life.[4] Sometimes mothers might even feel pressured by their doctors to abort after receiving a diagnosis of a genetic abnormality. In other countries, sex-selective abortion due to a preference for male children is common for those who can afford it. In addition, with more women delaying marriage and pregnancy into their mid to late thirties, the risk of genetic abnormalities is higher.

The viability of a child outside of the womb is another moving target, due to scientific and medical advances. Once a death sentence, babies born before twenty-six weeks' gestation now frequently survive, thanks to the development of treatments that keep lungs from collapsing and steroids that promote growth.[5] While babies born as early as twenty-two weeks *can* survive with good outcomes, most do not, or survive with permanent health problems and disabilities. Obviously, the functional viability of a life depends on where and when a baby is born and what kind of health care is accessible, but for now, the earliest possible viability happens to coincide closely with quickening, the informal marker of personhood in earlier eras. Certainly pregnancy and childbirth are safer now, and we can give thanks for the lives that have been saved by C-sections and neonatal intensive care units. But perhaps there is something in the movement back toward midwives and doulas that we can learn from: that women should be trusted with how they experience their own bodies and make medical decisions.

Though we know more than ever about reproduction, fetal development, and safe methods of abortion, questions remain. Neither science nor religion offers conclusive answers about when personhood begins. With fertilization? Implantation? Brain waves? A heartbeat? The ability to feel pain? The ability to survive outside the womb? The discussion of fetal personhood centers on the fetus, the embryo, even the fertilized egg—at the expense of the woman herself—hearkening back to those old images of woman as "host" and "soil."

The focus on the fetus at the expense of women has caused us to lose sight of women as full people with hopes and fears, dreams and desires, as people with the experience of their own bodies and emotions and their own health histories. The unborn child is easy to privilege; after all, she is innocent and uncomplicated, perfect fodder for all of our projections. A woman, however, is complicated and ripe for judgment for what she did or did not do. The predominant rhetoric in the abortion dialogue pits mothers against their own children—with phrases like "It's a child, not a choice"—rather than taking seriously the very real issues women face when bringing into the world a child, planned or unplanned.

As much as we scour history, science, politics, and a variety of religious traditions, there is no conclusive position on abortion or when personhood begins. Though verses from the Bible are frequently quoted in support of life beginning at conception, Scripture is rarely cut-and-dried, particularly when we bring modern questions, and interpretations vary. Nonetheless, as Christians, we hold the Bible as authoritative; so let us now turn to what the Bible says.

Chapter 4
WHAT THE BIBLE DOES (AND DOESN'T) SAY

For many Christians, the Bible is naturally the first place we turn to for guidance with a complicated issue, as Scripture is the ultimate authority for many Christian traditions. However, we also must remember that the Bible, in its complexity, was not written to answer the questions we bring before it in the twenty-first century, but to tell the story of the God of Israel and to testify to the revelation of that same God through Jesus Christ. The Bible contains poetry and proverbs, law and letters, etiologies and genealogies, and its myriad human authors, inspired but not dictated to by God, were more concerned with relaying divine truth than historical fact. This makes it much harder to proof-text, or select single verses out of context, to try to prove a particular point.

This is not to say that Scripture is not relevant to the debate on abortion. Many antiabortion activists are driven by their Christian faith, stating their convictions about "right to life" and "life beginning at conception" in the language of faith rather than political language. They appeal to the Bible more often than to the Constitution and the right to privacy that formed the basis of the Supreme Court decision in *Roe v. Wade*. So, if we are reading the same Bible, how can there be faithful Christians who are both antiabortion and proabortion rights? That difference lies in how we approach the authority of the Bible and through what lens we use to read it.

In this chapter, I will first address some of the individual verses that many Christians against legal abortion use to support their position, namely, that from the moment of conception an embryo is a human being and contains a soul, therefore making abortion akin to murder. From there, we will go beyond the Bible, looking at the ethics that underlie "pro-life" and "pro-choice" positions. To finish the chapter, we will look at how reading the Bible through a broadly pro-life, pro–human-flourishing hermeneutic or lens might help us rethink our labels and categories.

HOW DO ANTIABORTION
CHRISTIANS USE SCRIPTURE?

Often, when having a discussion with a person opposed to abortion, the first line of Scripture that he or she will quote is part of Psalm 139:

> For it was you who formed my inward parts;
> you knit me together in my mother's womb.
> I praise you, for I am fearfully and wonderfully made.
> Wonderful are your works;
> that I know very well.
> My frame was not hidden from you,
> when I was being made in secret,
> intricately woven in the depths of the earth.
> Your eyes beheld my unformed substance.
> In your book were written
> all the days that were formed for me,
> when none of them as yet existed.
>
> Ps. 139:13–16

This is a beautiful and moving section from an amazing psalm, easily one of my favorites to read and pray whenever I feel distant from God and in need of comfort. It is a prayer and a poem, characterized as a lament or a prayer for deliverance from personal enemies. It also ends with a plea for God to "kill the wicked" and "that the bloodthirsty would depart from me." Like many of the psalms, it contains a range of human emotions and language to communicate the truth that God is a personal God who knows each one of us intimately, loves us deeply, and has a plan for us. The New Testament corollary might be Jesus in Luke 12:7 telling the crowds, "But even the hairs of your head are all counted. Do not be afraid; you are of more value than many sparrows."

Quoting the psalms literally rather than reading or praying them as the hymnbook and prayer book of ancient Israel does a great disservice to the psalms themselves and how we interpret Scripture. If we take that passage literally, should we also then take Psalm 137:9 literally when the psalmist prays for vengeance, saying, "Happy shall they be who take your little ones and dash them against the rock"? Even when speaking of our enemies, Christians generally do not advocate infanticide.

It is highly unlikely that the author of Psalm 139 wrote verses 13–16 to address when life begins or the moral status of a fertilized egg, zygote, or fetus. The language and imagery that surround these verses makes a point about God as almighty and loving Creator. Earlier in the psalm, the author speaks of God's presence with him even "if I make my bed in Sheol" or "if I take the wings of the morning and settle at the farthest limits of the sea" (Ps. 139:8–9). It is a rhetorical device to demonstrate the depth and breadth of God's love and presence. Likewise, verses 13–16 are poetry that tell us that God is the all-knowing Creator of everything that is, not a literal, objective statement about the personhood of an embryo or fetus.

Antiabortion Christians also turn to Jeremiah 1:4–5, which contains similar language about God knowing an individual before he or she was even in the womb. "Now the word of the LORD came to me saying, 'Before I formed you in the womb I knew you, and before you were born I consecrated you; I appointed you a prophet to the nations.'" Again, this language can also be interpreted as the author using a rhetorical device to emphasize Jeremiah's selection as a prophet. Like the passage from Psalm 139, these verses from Jeremiah say more about the all-being and all-knowing characteristics of God than they say about the personhood of an embryo or fetus in the womb. Additionally, applying these verses broadly to every individual, born and unborn, is reading something into the text that is not there. Certainly God has not appointed everyone as a prophet to the nations; rather, these verses apply specifically to Jeremiah and his mission and vocation as a prophet of God.

Some Christians looking to Scripture to prove that God will punish those involved in abortions quote Amos 1:13: "Thus says the LORD: For three transgressions of the Ammonites, and for four, I will not revoke the punishment; because they have ripped open pregnant women in Gilead in order to enlarge their territory." Once again, context is key. Amos is prophesying the judgment and destruction of Israel's neighbors, including Edom, Tyre, Gaza, and Damascus in addition to the Ammonites. These other nations will be punished for various brutalities and ruthless war tactics. Therefore, these nations are wicked and will be punished by God.

Amos continues prophesying for several chapters, portending the transgressions of the nations and their

punishments by God. The reference to ripping open pregnant women is not a reference to surgical abortion, chosen
by a woman herself and performed by licensed profession-
als, but to the horrific cruelties of war and battle. Ideally
women and children, the elderly, and other noncombatants
should be protected from the horrors of battle, though such
atrocious actions as those committed by the Ammonites
and condemned in Scripture were probably not uncommon. While these verses do have something to say about
the horrors of warfare, they are not relevant to our discussion on abortion.

Moving to the New Testament and particularly the
Gospels, people looking to prove that Scripture proves the
personhood of the fetus turn to the encounter, directly after
Gabriel's annunciation, between Mary, the mother of Jesus,
and Elizabeth, the mother of John the Baptist, in the Gospel
of Luke. "In those days, Mary set out and went with haste
to a Judean town in the hill country, where she entered the
house of Zechariah and greeted Elizabeth. When Elizabeth
heard Mary's greeting, the child leaped in her womb. And
Elizabeth was filled with the Holy Spirit" (Luke 1:39–41).
This passage records John the Baptist kicking in the womb—
something many expectant mothers have experienced—
which Elizabeth, inspired by the Holy Spirit, then uses to
prophesy the birth of the Messiah. If Elizabeth feels John
move, she is beyond the point of quickening, likely past the
twenty-week mark of her pregnancy, far beyond when most
abortions—spontaneous or induced—occur. Additionally,
John the Baptist's situation, like that of Jeremiah, is a very
special one: as the one chosen to herald the arrival of the
Christ. Using these several verses about these particular
characters as some sort of proof of the personhood of an
unborn child from conception is, at best, a stretch.

Ultimately, we come back to the Ten Command-
ments, and the particular commandment "You shall not
murder" (Exod. 20:13). If someone believes in fetal personhood from the moment of conception, then abortion should
be considered murder, and murder is prohibited. Despite
the clarity of the commandment, other forms of killing, such
as warfare and capital punishment, are clearly authorized for
Israel. Is killing in self-defense a violation of this commandment? Obviously, there are exceptions and circumstances
that make this issue more complicated. When we approach
the Bible with these specific questions, we seem to come
away with only unsatisfactory and vague answers.

The closest a biblical reference comes to address-
ing the status of a child in the womb may be in Exodus
21:22, which is used by both antiabortion activists and
reproductive-rights activists: "When people who are fighting injure a pregnant woman so that there is a miscarriage,
and yet no further harm follows, the one responsible shall
be fined what the woman's husband demands, paying as
much as the judges determine." But then the law continues, stating, "If any harm follows, then you shall give life
for life, eye for eye, tooth for tooth, hand for hand, foot for
foot, burn for burn, wound for wound, stripe for stripe"
(Exod. 21:23–25). In other words, a miscarriage caused by
an individual is only worthy of a fine, while injury to the
mother is deserving of equal injury in kind. At least in terms
of Old Testament case law, the life of the pregnant woman
is considered more valuable than what is in her womb.

Even if we argue that this passage proves definitively
that the Bible is pro-choice, that a mother's life supersedes
that of a fetus in utero, we still come up against issues of
context, of the culture and time period in which this was
written. In this same section of Scripture, if an owner

merely injures rather than kills a slave by striking him or her with a rod, the owner suffers no penalty, because the slave is the owner's property (Exod. 20:20–21). As modern-day Christians, we would not use this passage to argue that slavery is somehow good or necessary or that beating a slave with a rod is not that bad, since Scripture states that the owner is not to be punished if the slave survives the beating (at least, I hope not!). Our broader consideration of the arc of salvation and our understanding of human dignity based on our Christian faith lead us to condemn slavery. Likewise, we may see the devaluing of the fetus as a similar issue of human dignity and civil rights. These are the challenges and the pitfalls of looking to individual verses and passages of Scripture to help prove what we already think to be true.

Instead of spitting out the various Bible verses that each side uses to "prove" that they are right, we would be better off to turn to Ecclesiastes 11:5: "Just as you do not know how the breath comes to the bones in the mother's womb, so you do not know the work of God, who makes everything," or Isaiah 55:8–9: "For my thoughts are not your thoughts, nor are your ways my ways, says the LORD. For as the heavens are higher than the earth, so are my ways higher than your ways and my thoughts than your thoughts." We should remember God's response out of the whirlwind to Job, who also approaches God expecting cut-and-dried answers to his questions. Rather than answering Job's questions, God questions Job, "Where were you when I laid the foundation of the earth? Tell me if you have understanding" (Job 38:4). Ultimately, Job repents by saying, "Therefore I have uttered what I did not understand, things too wonderful for me, which I did not know" (Job 42:3). Scripture is to be read and lived, argued with and

prayed in community. To demand that an ancient collection of sacred texts answer clearly and cleanly our moral
and ethical quandaries in the twenty-first century is to be
like Job shouting at a whirlwind.

FINDING SCRIPTURAL COMMON GROUND

While Christians on either side of the abortion debate may
disagree on the precise meaning of individual verses and
even on how we read the Bible, we still share a belief in
Scripture and Jesus Christ as the revelations of God. Similarly, while we also may disagree on the moral standing of a
developing prenatal child, we do share a common grounding in the Bible. We can read the biblical story together as
a pro-life story, as a testimony to the pro-life character of
God. Looking at the biblical arc, we can agree across the
aisle that God is for life over death, for freedom over slavery, and for human flourishing over all kinds of oppression—social, legal, political, economic, and religious.

Our biblical story begins with creation, an act of
giving life. God loves into being everything that is, including humankind, but we separate ourselves from God and
go astray. Through a series of covenants, God promises
to bless the whole earth through the descendants of Abra-
ham. When God's people fall into slavery in Egypt and are
undergoing great suffering, God acts through Moses for
the purposes of their liberation. Again and again, God's
people fall away from God and reject God, but God continues to seek out God's people and sends prophets and
kings to help restore the relationship. Eventually, out of
love for God's creation, God becomes incarnate through
Jesus Christ to redeem the world. Jesus lives out God's

mission of love and reconciliation through his teaching, his miracles of healing, his feeding ministry, and his sharp indictments of those who oppress the poor, the widows, and the orphans. Ultimately, this ministry upsets enough people that Jesus is handed over to and crucified by the Roman government.

However, this is not the end. In the decisive revelation of God's pro-life character, Jesus is raised from the dead—resurrected, not merely resuscitated. The stone has been rolled away, and the tomb is empty. Death has been destroyed and no longer has any power. After Jesus' ascension to heaven, when he is no longer with the disciples, they receive the gift of the Holy Spirit. The hope of salvation, of resurrection, is opened even to the Gentiles, and we anxiously await and pray for the coming of the kingdom of God in its fullness.

Creation, liberation, relationship, salvation, and resurrection are the fruits of God's power for life. We see these fruits in Jesus' own ministry as he restores people to health, not just in body but in spirit and community. The root word for "salvation" is the Latin *salus*, meaning health. Salvation is wholeness. What stronger statement can be made in favor of life than God's raising Jesus from the dead, evidence of God's power of life over death? And through Christ, we are all made truly alive. In John's Gospel, Jesus promises not just life but *abundant* life: "I came that they may have life, and have it abundantly," contrasted with the thief, who comes only to steal, kill, and destroy (John 10:10). Life in God is not merely existence, breathing and having a beating heart, but meaning and purpose and blessing. Abundant life is about flourishing.

While we may depart from our antiabortion brothers and sisters on issues like when a prenatal child becomes a person, and whether abortion, in all cases, is murder, we do share common ground in the resurrected Christ and the promises of an abundant life in him. Like the psalmist in Psalm 139, we believe that God intimately knows and loves all of God's creation and that we cannot escape that love, no matter where we go or what we do. We also agree that, even as the kingdom of God was partially inaugurated with the resurrection, we are still living in a sinful and fallen world, full of tragedy and heartbreak. The kingdom of God has not yet been fully established; so, everywhere we turn, we face brokenness.

We all read Scripture through a certain lens, what scholars call a hermeneutic. We bring our own questions, experiences, and theology to the text, which leads us to privilege certain stories, verses, and even books over others, no matter whether we identify as pro-choice or anti-abortion. There is no such thing as an unbiased reader. As Christians, we are taught to read the Bible, even the Old Testament, through the lens of the life, death, and resurrection of Jesus Christ. God's pro-life action through Christ trumps other stories of when God has been the dealer of death, such as in the tenth plague, when all the firstborn sons in Egypt are struck down (Exod. 12:12), because it is part of God's plan for salvation of the world through Israel.

The political realities of our day tell us that being pro-life and pro-choice are incompatible, but as Christians, we should all be pro-life, in favor of that abundant life that Jesus came to give us. We see the hallmarks of that abundant life in Jesus' ministry of feeding and healing and in his example of loving God and loving neighbor. Through our baptisms, we are baptized into that ministry as well, but when we look around at our communities and our world, we see suffering. We see children who go to bed hungry, schools without adequate resources, and families who work hard and still struggle to purchase basic necessities. We see a world at war, at home in our communities where gun violence is prevalent and abroad. We are so far from the kingdom that Isaiah prophesies, where "the wolf shall live with the lamb, the leopard shall lie down with the kid, the calf and the lion and the fatling together, and a little child shall lead them" (Isa. 11:6).

An abundant life for women includes being able to plan her family with her partner and having access to the health care that helps them do so. Both pro-choice and antiabortion Christians can see abortion as a tragedy, while acknowledging the economic realities that require women to choose between parenting another child and making a living. However, many who call themselves antiabortion also fight access to affordable contraception, which calls into question whether this fight is really about birthing children or controlling women's bodies. Some states even have laws that criminalize women who use drugs while pregnant, lowering the chance that these women will seek the help and health care they so desperately need.

Women terminated pregnancies before *Roe v. Wade*, and they will continue to seek abortions if it is ever overturned; the issue is whether those abortions will be safe and accessible, particularly for women on the margins with few resources. A pro-life ethic based on God's action in Scripture demands that we consider the fullness of life from birth until death, the possibility of human flourishing and not just human existence. While we bemoan the tragic nature of abortion, vilifying women for their choices, in many cases this decision is born out of the other ways in which our world is broken and sinful. Being pro-choice is not an automatic rubber stamp for abortions, but we are naive if we fail to acknowledge the consequences of outlawing abortion on the health and well-being of half of the population.

It is for this reason that the official position of many mainline Christian denominations is pro-choice, which we will turn to in the next chapter.

Chapter 5
PRO-CHOICE CHURCHES?

Since many people associate Christianity with an antichoice position, they might be surprised that Christian clergy have long been active in facilitating a woman's right to choose. Even before the Supreme Court decision in *Roe v. Wade*, clergy formed an underground network in response to the deaths and injuries of women caused by unsafe abortions and predatory abortion providers. The Clergy Consultation Service (CCS), established in 1967, helped to refer women to safe abortion providers. Many of the clergy initially involved had been active in the civil rights movement during the 1960s and connected their theological positions on race and dignity to their commitment to helping women and their families gain safe access to abortion. In the wake of the Supreme Court's decision on *Roe v. Wade* in 1973, CCS morphed into the Religious Coalition for Abortion Rights, consisting of several Protestant denominations and other faith traditions.

Since 1993, this group has been known as the Religious Coalition for Reproductive Choice (RCRC). Its current mission statement proclaims that it values and promotes religious liberty and "upholds the human and constitutional rights of all people to exercise their conscience to make their own reproductive health decisions without shame and stigma." On its website, it proudly supports not only safe, legal abortion services regardless of income or circumstance but also additional issues relevant to reproductive choices, like access to comprehensive sexuality education, family planning and contraception, affordable child care and health care, and support for and access to adoption services. Front and center on its home page in large letters we read, "Pro Faith, Pro Family, Pro Choice."

Perhaps it is not a surprise that clergy from a variety of faith traditions saw a consistent ethic connecting social and cultural changes in the 1960s and 1970s—the civil rights movement, the ordination of women in several traditions and denominations, and reproductive freedom. Despite comprising a variety of theological traditions and faiths, the constituents of RCRC claim their work stems from convictions held in common, namely, "compassion and love for others and the dignity of all people regardless of color or sex." These are theological convictions that promote a particular theological anthropology, not just a political conviction derived from interpreting the Constitution. In other words, the members of the RCRC are pro-choice *because of* their faith, not *in spite of* it.

The broader public might be shocked to know that so many religious organizations and denominations are members of a pro-choice consortium, as those who are against abortion often claim their position as the only acceptable faith-based one. In recent years, liberal-leaning denominations have been vocal on issues like racial reconciliation, welcoming refugees, economic inequality, and protecting Native American land from oil pipelines, yet they have been oddly quiet about reproductive choice, even as many state legislatures have sought to limit access. This silence may have cost the pro-choice movement some allies, as conservative Christians have dominated the conversation.

At its May 2016 General Conference, the United Methodist Church voted to withdraw from RCRC, despite being one of the founding members in 1973. The UMC's involvement in RCRC has been discussed and debated at General Conferences since 2004. The petition cited disagreement with the coalition's position on abortion, namely, gender-selection abortions and late-term abortions. Even though no church dollars funded RCRC, and RCRC itself recognizes that the views of member denominations or organizations vary, the UMC felt that it needed to break ties. Some argued that, despite disagreements, the UMC needed to remain at the table in order to influence RCRC positively to represent their particular United Methodist social principles. The Rev. Beth Ann Cook from the Indiana Conference stated, "Our United Methodist Church has a carefully nuanced official position on the difficult issue of abortion. It is not as strong as some of us would like nor as clearly pro-choice as others would like. [The RCRC] is neither nuanced nor moderate." A few months later, several individual conferences within the UMC, including the Oregon-Idaho, California-Nevada, New England, New York, and Pacific Northwest conferences, voted to join RCRC.[1]

The conflict within the United Methodist Church demonstrates the variety of perspectives on abortion and other social issues that exist in many denominations. Some members may be shocked and surprised to learn that their denomination has developed a statement or resolution in favor of a woman's access to reproductive choice, including abortion. Rarely do those who support these statements speak from the pulpit in the same enthusiastic way as Christians who believe that abortion is murder and urge their congregations to vote only for the antiabortion candidate. Neither have they been as debated in recent years as other issues around sexuality, like LGBTQI marriage and ordi-nation. As Daniel Maguire points out in his book *Sacred Choices*, the "statements from the denominations [about abortion] are clear. Unfortunately, they haven't been loud, and a lot of people and politicians have never heard them."[2]

Denominational statements on social issues like abortion raise questions of what kind of authority church-wide structures have to make these statements, especially denominations that lack a strong centralized authority. If I am a United Methodist, and I disagree with the United Methodist position on abortion, that does not make me any less of a United Methodist. As the denomination's web-site states, "[The Church's statements] are intended to be instructive and persuasive, but they are not church law and are not binding on members. Members will hold differing views on abortion. There is no requirement for members to agree with the Church's view."[3] It is certainly easier to demand that women not have abortions than it is to demand that women prayerfully discern their reproductive choices along with those affected by them.

Denominational statements vary in their language and their focus. Many, like the 1988 statement from the General Board of American Baptist Churches, recognize the diversity of viewpoints among their membership, point-ing out, "Many of our membership seek legal safeguards to protect unborn life. Many others advocate for and support family planning legislation, including legalized abortion as in the best interest of women in particular and society in general. . . . Consequently, we acknowledge the freedom of each individual to advocate for a public policy on abortion that reflects his or her beliefs."[4]

Others focus on the separation of church and state and the right to religious freedom. For example, the Disciples of Christ General Assembly in 1975 and 1989 resolved to "respect differences in religious beliefs concerning abortion and oppose, in accord with the principle of religious liberty, any attempt to legislate a specific religious opinion or belief concerning abortion upon all Americans."[5] Regardless of the multiplicity of views and perspectives among Christians on abortion, Christianity is not the established religion in the United States of America; therefore laws should not side with one religious position against the other. Similarly, as Maguire points out, law requires an underlying consensus, and just because Christians might think something immoral, doesn't mean that it should be illegal.[6] Our national history with outlawing alcohol during Prohibition is a good example of what can happen when laws do not have an underlying consensus.

These statements from mainline Protestant denominations like the Episcopal Church, the Presbyterian Church (USA), the United Church of Christ, and the Evangelical Lutheran Church in America vary in how they see legal abortion fit into a faith-based framework. The UCC's statement from the Eighth General Synod in 1971 (pre-*Roe v. Wade!*) is perhaps the most fleshed out theologically, weighing our God-given freedom with a reverence for human life and even going so far as to tackle some of the arguments about when life begins, with the options including conception, implantation, fixing of the genetic code (three weeks), first central nervous system activity (eight weeks), brain development and cardiac activity (twelve weeks), the moment of quickening, or viability (twenty to twenty-eight weeks).[7] The statement also includes a call to action for advocacy in repealing abortion restrictions and increasing access to sex education, contraception, and abortion. In subsequent years, the General Synod has added to these calls to action, particularly naming the discrepancy in access between the rich and the poor and condemning the Hyde Amendment, which blocks the use of federal funds for abortion.

Almost every denominational statement specifies when abortion is always a morally acceptable option. Most of these statements explicitly name situations like rape, incest, fetal abnormalities, and when there exists a danger to the life of the mother as carte blanche for pursuing an abortion, with the understanding, if not the blessing, of the church. These situations are traumatic enough without the condemnation of a woman's spiritual community. Even members of denominations that explicitly oppose abortion often will make an exception for these kinds of tragic scenarios. The Southern Baptist Convention's Resolution on the Partial-Birth Abortion Ban in 1996 that "all abortions, except in those very rare cases where the life of the mother is clearly in danger, are wrong," allows for exception, however carefully qualified.[8] In several statements, a woman facing an unplanned pregnancy is urged seriously and prayerfully to consider alternative options, like adoption or the child being raised by a family member, before pursuing an abortion.

Likewise, many of these statements state very clearly what abortion should not be used for. The United Methodist Church explicitly names using abortion as a means of gender selection as unacceptable and unethical, and the 1994 General Convention of the Episcopal Church passed a resolution deploring the practice of forced abortion and sterilization in the People's Republic of China.[9] Many denominations stress that abortion should not be undertaken as a means of birth control or a method of convenience. For example, the 1994 resolution from the General Convention of the Episcopal Church reads, "While we acknowledge that in this country it is the legal right of every woman to have a medically safe abortion, as Christians we believe strongly that if this right is exercised, it should be used only in extreme situations. We emphatically oppose abortion as a means of birth control, family planning, sex selection, or any reason of mere convenience."[10] Without a means of reversible contraception that is 100 percent effective, I think this sounds a little harsh, though I certainly agree that abortion should not be a *primary* means of birth control or family planning.

While various denominations may list when it is permissible to pursue an abortion and circumstances where it is discouraged, more and more situations lie in the middle ground, that gray area. So many of these statements seem to be written without ever talking to a woman who has contemplated or decided on abortion. There is rarely a mention of the implications of pregnancy, childbearing, and childrearing upon a woman's psychological, spiritual, and social health, in addition to her physical health. Nor do these statements address the role and responsibility of men and fatherhood. The condemnation of those who receive abortion out of "convenience," when it is usually anything but a convenience, sounds a lot like the condemnation of pro-choice politicians who are accused of advocating for "abortion on demand," as if it is something you can order up like a television movie or Chinese takeout.

These statements also fail to distinguish between *discouraging* abortion for certain reasons and *legislating* those same reasons. For example, many of these statements discourage abortion for the purposes of sex selection, terminating a pregnancy based on the predicted sex of the infant (usually female children); and as cited above, sex-selective abortions were one reason that the United Methodist Church decided to withdraw its membership from the Religious Coalition for Reproductive Choice. Far from condoning sex-selective abortion, the fear from the RCRC and other reproductive-rights activists is that laws condemning sex-selective abortions sanction discrimination against women of Asian descent, who are seen as more likely to terminate pregnancies based on the child's predicted sex. Additionally, legislation of certain subjective conditions places a medical provider in the situation of trying to decide whether a woman is getting an abortion for "right" or "wrong" reasons.

Many of the statements from mainline denominations appear to be attempting to defend a woman's right to choose by using the same starting place and logic as those who are antiabortion—the personhood of the unborn. I cannot imagine that we will ever be in a place to definitively name when life begins, regardless of scientific advances or medical technology, but it may forever be somewhere on a spectrum from the conception and implantation of an embryo to when a baby is viably delivered. Nevertheless, it is the fetus, the "innocent unborn" that is in the foreground—never the woman. What if we, as Christians in our denominational statements, started with women, as Katha Pollitt suggests: "What is the moral status of women? How much right to life do women have? How much personhood? What about *their* souls?"[11] The division between virtuous and unvirtuous abortions invites judgment upon women, most of whom are just trying to do their best in a world that has stacked the deck against them. The average heterosexual woman spends about thirty years managing her fertility, which necessitates time, money, and effort—trips to the pharmacy, doctor's appointments, and so on—all for methods of birth control that are not 100 percent effective, and yet ill-timed or unwanted pregnancies are treated as a small thing, as if despite our best efforts, women should still be prepared to bear and raise children at any moment, at least if we're engaging in sexual activity.

Notably, most of the statements supporting a woman's right to a safe, legal abortion are several decades old, almost as if the mainline position has thrown up its hands and ceded this ground to the Roman Catholic Church and more theologically and politically conservative evangelical and fundamentalist churches. It is so personal, so morally ambiguous and fraught, such a third rail, that it's rarely discussed even in more progressive Christian circles. I attended a notoriously liberal divinity school that prided itself on a commitment to social justice, but there was virtually never a mention of abortion or reproductive rights except in passing. We discussed human sexuality and same-sex marriage in our ethics class—but not abortion. We were taught how to minister to victims of intimate-partner violence in our pastoral care class—but not how to counsel someone facing a difficult or unplanned pregnancy.

Even as mainline denominations make statements in favor of other justice issues—like LGBTQI rights, an end to the death penalty, sensible gun legislation, and support for racial justice organizations like Black Lives Matter—they remain remarkably silent on issues of reproductive justice. With political attacks on abortion rights and threats to defund Planned Parenthood, these churches, in trying to protect a woman's access to reproductive care, don't want to risk looking as if they are "proabortion" rather than "prowoman" or "pro-choice." Despite progressive politics and stances, even liberal-leaning churches still wrestle profoundly with sexism. While women have served as ordained clergy in some of these denominations for over forty years, only recently has there been any effort to address the gap in pay between male and female clergy and to institute maternity-leave policies. If the church is intended to model for society what gender equality looks like, it is not doing a very good job.

Perhaps this silence is born out of a recognition that there is indeed a tragic dimension to abortion, not necessarily located in the choice of an individual but in the society surrounding her. As the statement from the Episcopal Church reads, "We regard all abortion as having a tragic dimension, calling for the concern and compassion of all the Christian community."[12] The way that the church understands it, abortion should not be undertaken lightly even if it is clearly the right decision for that individual. This is juxtaposed with viewpoints like that of author and journalist Caitlin Moran, who stated that her decision to have an abortion was "quite easy," akin to a decision on coloring her hair.[13] In Moran's book *How to Be a Woman*, she pushes back against the myth that choosing an abortion is a uniquely agonizing decision, but perhaps goes too far toward flippancy. In her article "The Myth of Abortion Regret," Ruth Graham writes about a study in the journal *Contraception* that shows that women choosing abortion are more certain than those facing reconstructive knee surgery.[14]

Even the most vehemently antiabortion politicians and activists rarely argue for punishment of the women, instead targeting abortion providers, but this also proves that women are not making these decisions in a vacuum. Perhaps as Christians we can locate the tragic dimension of abortion in a society that routinely fails to value and protect women and families, which may or may not culminate in an individual woman's choice about whether to bear a child at a particular time. Let us locate the tragic dimension of abortion in a world that has fallen so far from what God intended—a world where one in five women is sexually assaulted in college but 63 percent of victims decline even to report to law enforcement and be revictimized by blaming and shaming,[15] a world where one in ten women report being raped by an intimate partner. Sexual violence, incest, and rape certainly constitute the experience of many women.

Using our religious imagination, we can try to conceive of a different world, one that has not fallen so far from what God intended, where every conceived child is desired and every pregnancy is met with joy. Before writing off this ideal as impossible, we can work toward a world without sexual violence—rape, incest, and abuse—and where sexual acts between two people are mutually characterized by delight, joy, and pleasure; a world where children are welcomed with love and care and take their place in households and communities that are empowered to meet everyone's physical, emotional, spiritual, and cultural needs. In this world, the flourishing of children and their families and communities are intertwined.

The evidence of our social and political realities shows that we are far from living in this ideal world. Thus women need safe, legal, and accessible options for terminating pregnancies. Yes, there is a tragic dimension to the loss of potential life, but it is borne by all of us, not just the individual woman making the decision. It is a tragedy and a sin that is part and parcel of the system we exist in, which diminishes both potential and extant life. We all should repent and work toward a better, broader world.

The role of the church and its ministers in this debate and reality for many women should be to offer support, counsel, and guidance. Too often women and their partners have experienced judgment, shame, and guilt from the church. These matters are intensely personal and, for the Christian, spiritual. Some women may feel the need to confess or do penance for their decision, while others may feel traumatized in other ways.

Familiarizing ourselves with the official statements from our denomination of preference is a starting point for thinking theologically but also pastorally about abortion and reproductive rights. We might find ourselves in agreement with the position or in disagreement. We may wish that the statements went further or think that they go too far. Wrapped up in the abortion debate are complex and complicated theological ideas about bodies, freedom, and life, not to mention sex, families, and parenthood. Very likely, we might find ourselves certain that we would never make the choice to terminate a pregnancy but willing to defend someone else's legal right to make that choice.

While we work to make abortion rare, we should also ensure that it remains safe, in that it is offered by a licensed medical professional, accessible regardless of economic or geographic circumstances, and legal. We cannot forget that the members of the Religious Coalition for Reproductive Choice banded together because of the horror of what was happening to women who sought illegal abortions. Helping women access needed reproductive care, including abortion, is a social justice issue in which the church as the gathered body of Christ can play an important role.

The Role of the Church

Most people do not view the church as a safe space in which they could talk about issues of sex, sexuality, and reproduction, including abortion. Like many young adults, I was raised with the message from school and church that I should remain sexually abstinent until marriage. Growing up, I didn't feel that the church was a place in which I could realistically wrestle with issues of sexuality. So much of our discourse lately in progressive mainline churches has focused on sexual orientation and same-sex marriage, but we still often fail to address sexual development and decision making with young people.

The "purity culture" era did a lot of damage to a lot of people, especially to women who suffered sexual assault and violence and were taught that they were "damaged goods." When 90 to 95 percent of people have sex before marriage (and in cases of divorce, outside of marriage), how can the church speak to that reality?[16] For a book that explores sex and desire from a Christian perspective and promotes an ethical view of sex, I recommend Bromleigh McCleneghan's *Good Christian Sex*. Just because someone is in a monogamous marital relationship does not mean the sex is ethical. Rape occurs within marriage. Abuse occurs within marriage. Marriage alone does not meet the condition for ethical sex within a Christian framework.

The church does not have a great track record for talking about sex, but it does have a long history of profound discomfort with sex, in part because of its low view of women. Women are either virgins or mothers or whores. Women are bifurcated into holiness or prostitution. This has bled into the broader American culture, in which sex is omnipresent in advertisements and television and movie entertainment, but is still broadly seen as something shameful and dirty. We are part of what Jill Filipovic calls a "sex-obsessed but pleasure-starved culture."[17] In this culture, we don't have the incentives or the tools to plan for sex or take positive responsibility for making healthy choices.

Perhaps the church can still preach the importance of marriage and hold that sexual fulfillment and intimacy are most fully realized within the commitment of marriage, while recognizing that we are no longer in a society that marries off girls as soon as they start menstruating. As both women and men forestall marriage and childbearing into their thirties, the church has an opportunity to provide a moral and ethical sexual framework that is not provided by the broader society. This could serve to strengthen marriages by helping couples talk openly about their needs and desires. Talking upfront about sexuality, contraceptive plans, and the possibility of dealing with unplanned pregnancies is difficult, but if the church takes the incarnation seriously, it should be a safe place to bring our whole selves, including our sexuality.

My hope is that the church would be a place where women facing unplanned pregnancies and women who have chosen abortions could come and feel safe expressing their doubts and fears as well as their joys and hopes. If the church is not able to walk with people through challenging and distressing times in their lives, then what good is it? When clergy and educated lay leaders are not trained to talk about reproductive health care, including abortion, it is difficult to be a pastoral presence for women in difficult situations. How can clergy care for the one in three women who will have an abortion by age forty if we never talk about it? How can we pray with and for a woman facing an unplanned or unwanted pregnancy without being coercive if we do not learn? These are volatile and intensely personal issues, but if the church wants to remain relevant, we must be present in people's lives and available for when they seek the counsel of clergy and the church.

The church, as a bearer of a pro-life ethos, should not encourage abortion, nor should it heap on the shame and disdain for women that the outside world does. The church and its surrogates should accompany, bear witness to, support, and pray with women throughout their decision-making process. If necessary and desired, the church should offer forgiveness and grace. One of the pastoral outcomes of Pope Francis's Year of Mercy is his commitment to extend the ability of priests (and not only bishops) to forgive abortion. While this does not contradict the Catholic belief that abortion is a horrible sin, it does recognize that good, moral people (even Catholics) get abortions. It positions the church and its clergy as vehicles of grace and mercy instead of providers of punishment and shame.

As an Episcopalian, I am thankful that I come from a liturgical tradition with beautifully written prayers and worship resources. The 1979 *Book of Common Prayer* contains prayers in thanksgiving for the birth of a child; more recently, liturgical resources were published in 2009 for situations involving childbearing, childbirth, and loss. *Rachel's Tears, Hannah's Hopes* includes prayers and liturgies for blessing, lament, repentance, and reconciliation after abortion. It covers a broad range of feelings that women and their partners might experience around childbirth and childbearing: joy, fear, uncertainty, anger, grief, hope. The rite of repentance and reconciliation even includes space for the woman to share her story in the middle of reading Scripture, asking forgiveness, and being absolved. The rubrics also specify that the language can be changed for men who come seeking repentance for their role in an abortion. Other denominations might develop similar liturgical resources for use.

Given the simplistic dialogue that continues to equate "Christian" with "antiabortion rights," the presence of churches advocating for reproductive rights seems counterintuitive, but reproductive care is an integral part of the lives of women and their families. It is an issue in line with the proenvironment, antiracism, antipoverty positions the church has already proclaimed. We must expand the definition of "pro-life" beyond the life of the fetus to circumstances that promote and encourage the flourishing of all people. If we want to be pro-life as God is pro-life, then we must be pro–all life, including the lives of women, and reclaim that term from its narrow focus on abortion, our subject for the next chapter.

Chapter 6
REFRAMING PRO-LIFE AND FINDING COMMON GROUND

In his book *Beyond the Abortion Wars: A Way Forward for a New Generation*, Charles C. Camosy points out how problematic and unclear the categories of "pro-choice" and "pro-life" are. In fact, according to a 2011 Public Religion Research Institute poll, "[s]even-in-ten Americans say the term 'pro-choice' describes them somewhat or very well, and nearly two-thirds simultaneously say the term 'pro-life' describes them somewhat or very well."[1] Our current debate is structured so that it sets pro-life and pro-choice as opposites, two extremes, though according to that poll the waters are quite muddy, with around a third of people claiming both labels to some degree.

This language of "pro-choice" and "pro-life" divides and obscures, because, when we drill down to what we believe, we see that people hold more in common than they might think. After all, who among us would not want to see and name ourselves as pro-life? The corollary to pro-life would seem to be pro-death, which would not accurately describe any normal person. Of course, extremes exist on both sides. There are those who identify as pro-life who would prefer to see abortion outlawed entirely, except maybe when there is a risk to the health of the mother. And there are those who identify as pro-choice who view abortion as an easy fix to the problem of an unwanted pregnancy.

In the 1996 Halloween-themed episode of *The Simpsons*, "Treehouse of Horror VII," two aliens, Kang and Kodos, disguised as Bill Clinton and Bob Dole, plot to conquer the world. It is a rather incisive commentary on American electoral politics in general. In a stump speech Kang, as Bob Dole, tackles the issue of abortion. He declares, "Abortions for all," and the crowd boos. He switches his position by saying, "Very well, no abortions for anyone," and again the crowd boos. Searching for the middle ground, he finally declares, "Hmm . . . Abortions for some, miniature American flags for others," and the crowd erupts into cheers as they wave miniature American flags. Obviously, the intention of this scene is humorous, but it illustrates how extremes are neither popular nor effective when it comes to the issue of abortion.

While many people who support abortion rights would say they support "life," meaning the flourishing of all people, there can still be a negative reaction to those who classify themselves as "pro-life" because of how that phrase gets used politically—usually in relationship to overturning *Roe v. Wade* (which would only thrust the abortion debate onto the states)—or in equating abortion with murder. "Pro-life" often appears to really mean "pro-birth," as politicians restrict reproductive access while also cutting the social safety net that would help provide for women and children.

However, people who identify as pro-life on the issue of abortion have a variety of stances and beliefs. Some identify that way because they view life as beginning before viability. Others identify as "pro-life" because they would like to see a decrease in the rate of abortion and earnestly believe they would never choose it for themselves. A few politicians like Catholic Democratic senator Tim Kaine consider themselves personally pro-life, but politically pro-choice, in that they are not seeking to legislate their personal and religious beliefs with regard to abortion.

THE QUESTION OF FETAL PERSONHOOD

Those who oppose abortion frequently use phrases like "life begins at conception" or "the fetus is a human being." But what do those mean? To delve into these issues more deeply, we must first answer questions about how we define "life" and "a human being." At first, this may seem ridiculous; after all, don't we know it when we see it? We may be categorizing a fetus as a member of the species Homo sapiens based on DNA, or we may be giving it a moral status, which, Charles Camosy says, "makes it more or less wrong to kill or otherwise harm."[2]

How we understand life differs, depending upon species and stage of development. Most of us have no societal qualms about chopping down a tree for firewood or eating some animals for food (though we may have ethical qualms about mass deforestation and factory farming) even though, in both of those cases, a life is ended. And yes, by a strict definition, a fertilized egg is biologically alive; its cells reproduce and it has the basic building blocks to become a human being. If we consider the development of a human child from conception to birth, it is evident that there is a huge change from the fertilization and implantation of an egg to the birth of a human child who is viable outside the womb. Somewhere along that continuum, the prenatal child becomes recognizable and even viable as an independent person, not just a bundle of cells, perhaps with a recognizable head and tail.

Despite some of the rhetoric from antiabortion advocates, no one is advocating for abortions in the eighth or ninth month of pregnancy unless there is serious concern for the life of the mother or the child. In 2011, only 1.3 percent of abortions occurred after the twenty-one-week mark, with over 90 percent occurring in the first thirteen weeks of pregnancy.[3] It seems like common sense that preference would be for a woman to terminate a pregnancy sooner rather than later, if that is her decision. As the fetus develops, it becomes more and more recognizable as a human being, with a heartbeat, brain waves, and a capacity to feel pain, even as it is still dependent on sustenance and safety from its mother.

Unfortunately, sometimes the inaccessibility of abortion services due to geography, transportation, or cost pushes back the timeline of terminating a pregnancy. A woman might not even know that she is pregnant until six or eight weeks into a pregnancy, and the high rate of early miscarriages in the first trimester further complicates whether we view a fetus in the earliest stages of development as a person with moral claims. There is no doubt that an early miscarriage of a planned pregnancy is a source of grief and pain for a family, but it differs in nature from a later miscarriage, a stillbirth, or the death of an infant or young child.

Hypothetically, somewhere between the fertilization of an egg and the birth of a child, a mass of cells becomes a person in the moral sense, with a right to life. Katha Pollitt uses the philosopher Joel Feinberg's term "common-sense person" as one who "thinks, feels, communicates, [and] has more-or-less human features."[4] This would include the mentally disabled, the ill, the elderly, even those in a permanent vegetative state who have a "residual social place"—relations, property, citizenship, etc.[5] However, these do not apply to a prenatal child in its early stages of development. We have some sense that a zygote is different from a five-year-old child in terms of her place in society and our moral responsibility to her.

At the same time, we might argue that, because we do not know when a person becomes a person, it is best and safest to act as if a fertilized egg is a person, to err on the side of life.[6] Because this zygote has the potential to be a human, it should receive special protections, in the way that groups of people who have been historically discriminated against based on race, gender, or sexual identity receive special protections. But consider this: If we cannot know for sure, perhaps we should rely instead on a woman—whose personhood is not in doubt—and her conscience as the one who is most affected.

This leads us to a discussion about freedom of conscience and the moral agency of women. "Trust women" was the slogan that pro-choice advocates used in the early days of fighting for reproductive rights, and it still rings true today. If science and religion cannot say conclusively when a fetus becomes a person, and if we believe the law protects a right to privacy that allows an individual to make choices about his or her own body, perhaps we should trust women to make these choices for themselves. Moral decision making is complex, and different women will come to different decisions based on their values, their economic standing, their relationships, and their health.

Privileging the moral agency of a woman over the prospective life of a fetus does not mean that we celebrate the decision to terminate a pregnancy. As Ann Furedi quotes Ronald Dworkin, "it is quite consistent to hold 'a profound conviction that it is intrinsically wrong deliberately to end a human life' and yet 'believe that a decision whether to end human life in early pregnancy must nevertheless be left to the pregnant woman whose conscience is most directly connected to the choice, and who has the greatest stake in it.'"[7] We can still hold that abortion is a tragedy, a loss, even a death of sorts, and do everything in our power to work toward a world in which women are less inclined to make that choice.

A primary example of this difficult moral decision making occurs with late-term abortions, which, despite their overwhelming condemnation in public discourse, are exceedingly rare and difficult to obtain except when there is a very real danger to the mother or the baby. Even then, prohibitive state laws may make it necessary for a woman to travel to receive adequate health care that meets her needs. When the topic came up in the 2016 debate between presidential candidates Donald Trump and Hillary Clinton, women took to the Internet to tell their stories of late-term abortions—namely, how emotionally and psychologically painful it was to lose a much-desired child and how difficult such abortions were to obtain.

The website Jezebel published the saga of "Elizabeth" and her abortion at thirty-two weeks of a baby she and her husband had desperately hoped for, only to learn about multiple complications that would render the baby incompatible with life upon delivery. Because of the laws in different states, Elizabeth ended up flying out to Colorado to receive an abortifacient injection and then returning to New York for a dilation and curettage (D&C). The whole story is tragic and awful to read, not least because of the hoops that she had to jump through to protect her own health and to minimize the suffering of her child.[8] Reading any of these first-person accounts of late-term abortion only emphasizes how difficult, rare, and expensive they are and leads the reader to sympathize with the woman. If anything, governmental regulations and restrictions only make these horrific situations harder for women and their families.

THE INHERENTLY TRAGIC NATURE OF ABORTION

As Christians who share Jesus' commitment to the poor, the vulnerable, and the oppressed, we can support a woman's right to exercise her own freedom of conscience in making moral decisions about her body and family and also acknowledge the tragic element present in any abortion. Along with our antiabortion brothers and sisters, we affirm the sanctity of life and want to do everything in our power to support that life from its conception to its end. Even if I might never make that choice for myself, I support my sister's right to choose based on her own circumstances. We share concerns about the potential eugenics abuses of abortion, for gender-selection or for eliminating any disability or survivable genetic anomaly. The possibilities of so-called "designer babies," genetically modified preferentially to choose gender or eye color, could lead to a dangerous and unethical slippery slope. When 90 percent of fetuses diagnosed with Trisomy 21 or Down syndrome are aborted, we are concerned. We believe that God created us beautiful in diversity, and children born with disabilities should move us to sympathy and protection, not elimination of differences.

We are also concerned about the broader devaluing of life that we see in our wider culture, particularly around people who are unable to be economically productive—the very young, the very old, and those with physical or mental disabilities. Much of our society passively treats these people as a burden to our common life, rather than with the respect and dignity that every human being deserves. On the other end of the life spectrum from abortion, there is a similar discussion about freedom of choice and life around euthanasia and whether one has the right to a medically assisted death, especially in the face of a disease diagnosis with the potential of great suffering. So far, six states in the United States have authorized medical aid in dying for patients facing a diagnosis of six months or less to live.

In many feminist circles, even to name abortion as a tragedy is controversial. If, after all, the fetus has no moral claim on us, then abortion is just another medical procedure, a regular part of a woman's reproductive life and health. Advocates for abortion rights see naming abortion as a tragedy akin to shaming women for seeking abortion; from there, it's a short step to calling a woman a murderer. But if we locate that tragedy in the broader system rather than in the individual choice of the woman, our intention is not to shame and blame her for the circumstances in which she finds herself. Abortion can be the best choice for a woman and her family and still be a tragedy. We might understand this a little bit like divorce. Divorce can be the right choice for a couple, and sometimes necessary in cases of abuse, addiction, or infidelity, but we still mourn the tragedy of it, our individual and collective fallen nature that makes an undesirable option the best option in a given scenario.

As we saw in the chapters on the history of abortion, discussions about reproductive rights, on both the right and the left, are not immune to racism and classism. Initial advocates of outlawing abortions wanted to encourage more white women to have babies, and our country has a history of forcibly sterilizing people of color and people with disabilities and mental illnesses. While no choice as important as bringing life into the world can be made in a vacuum, there is a danger of coercion, both direct and indirect. Women on the margins who may end up utilizing government programs for support if they have a child may be pressured to remain self-sufficient rather than go "on the dole." Middle- and upper-class parents of a young, single pregnant woman may encourage her to think of her future and how she will be "wasting" an education or a career if she gives birth out of wedlock. Despite the changing social norms around marriage and childbirth, many well-off families are reluctant to face the social stigmatization of their daughter's "accident."

All women need to be able to choose for themselves— black and brown women, drug-addicted women, working women, single women, women with no children, and women with five children. Our role is not to judge or condemn any particular individual's circumstances but to support life as the gift we believe it to be, however it comes to us.

The situations of individual women and their families occur not in a vacuum but in a broader system plagued by brokenness. It is a system afflicted by the sins of violence, patriarchy, white supremacy, and unfair distribution of wealth. It is a system that places more value on economic productivity than empathy. Women's need for abortion access is a symptom of these deeper, more ingrained sins of our society, and if we take God's pro-life mission seriously, our work as Christians will be to reduce abortions by fighting these deeper sins that afflict our common life and that see women, particularly women of color and LGBT women, as second-class citizens.

In naming God as pro-life, pro-choice Christians can also find common ground with antiabortion brothers and sisters in seeing this tragic dimension to every abortion. We can agree that it is tragic when a woman finds herself in a situation where abortion appears to be the best option, whether that situation is due to rape, incest, danger to the mother, the baby not being viable outside of the womb at birth, or economic or relationship concerns. It is tragic that our society is unwilling or unable to support the conditions necessary for both mother and child to flourish. Certainly, these situations are not what God desires for the creation and people that God loves so much.

ABUNDANT LIFE FOR ALL

A consistent pro-life Christian ethic should have as much to say about every death-dealing, antiflourishing scenario as it does about abortion, but too often those who label themselves "pro-life" for means of political expediency remain silent on other issues. To reference Sister Joan Chittister again, a consistent pro-life ethic would be as concerned with the quality of life of any particular child as it is with that child's birth, and we need a broader conversation on what that looks like. That ethic would address access to health care, housing, food, education, and safety. A broad pro-life ethic would be concerned with social justice issues of racism and sexism, homophobia, poverty, and refugees fleeing war and environmental disasters. All of these issues and more would fall under the umbrella "pro-life," based on what we as Christians know about God as revealed through Jesus Christ.

The whole arc of the biblical witness is an expansive pro-life statement, from the creation of the cosmos to the second coming of Christ with the replacement of the old earth with the new Jerusalem, wherein God comes to dwell with humanity and sin is ended. Whether we take a literal seven-day creationist view or a more mythological and eti-ological reading of the creation narratives in Genesis, our Scripture speaks to a fundamental truth for Christians: God created everything and, therefore, everything is God's. God is the source of light and life. It is in God that we live, move, and have our being (Acts 17:28). Even more so, as humans we are created in the very image of God. In Adam, we became subject to death, but in Christ, we are born into everlasting life. We have fallen into sin and away from rela-tionship with God, but through Christ we will be restored into that relationship for eternity.

If we say that we follow Jesus Christ, who has tri-umphed over death and the grave, then we must be broadly and passionately pro-life for all people, not just the unborn. Antiabortion advocates often specify that their passion is for the unborn because the unborn have no voice and are vulnerable; they often ignore the more complicated, less innocent vulnerable people living in our midst who are cry-ing out from oppression.

To be fair, there are segments of the Christian tradi-tion that are committed to a consistent pro-life ethic, affirm-ing the dignity and sacredness of all life, including unborn children. The more progressive wing of the Roman Catholic Church, including voices like those of Father James Mar-tin, SJ, and *America* magazine, have been openly critical of politicians who are antiabortion but then cut government assistance for those who most need it. They have spoken out against antilife policies like torture and in favor of renewed focus and dedication to refugees fleeing war and religious persecution. This "whole life" focus of the pro-life move-ment is a much-needed corrective to a term that for too long has been overly focused on a woman's womb to the detri-ment of other death-dealing policies that surround us.

From a medical perspective, when we consider everything that must go right for a child to be born, and all the different ways things can go wrong, life is indeed miraculous. But there is a difference between physical, biological life and life as the full expression of human potential. There are many scenarios in which we recognize the difference between biological existence and fulfillment. As we make our end-of-life plans, we consider "quality of life"—whether we would consider it acceptable to prolong our biological life with a respirator or feeding tube if we are no longer able to do the things we love or that have made life meaningful. Oftentimes, family members make decisions for loved ones, including young children, not to prolong life artificially and to minimize suffering when recovery is not likely. Even when these decisions are challenging, the primary concerns are quality of life and quality of death. Mothers who learn that their unborn child would most certainly suffer and die after birth are affected by these same concerns. Both in the secular and religious realms, we value other qualities as part of a fulfilled life; "life" concerns more than just existence.

The Christian conception of fulfillment or liberty or happiness is not merely pursuing that which gives us a fleeting sense of joy. "For freedom Christ has set us free," Paul writes in Galatians 5:1, in a discussion of whether they should follow the Jewish law. Paradoxically, our freedom is found in service, even slavery, to God. Jesus declares his mission to the world when he reads a section of Isaiah in the synagogue, "The Spirit of the Lord is upon me, because he has anointed me to bring good news to the poor. He has sent me to proclaim release to the captives and recovery of sight to the blind, to let the oppressed go free, to proclaim the year of the Lord's favor" (Luke 4:18–19). These are the conditions of life: good news to the poor, release to the captives, recovery of sight to the blind, letting the oppressed go free, and the proclamation of the jubilee year. These are not just spiritual realities, but physical realities as well: relief from economic poverty, freedom from captivity, and health for the sick. Jesus lives out this proclamation through his ministry of healing and feeding, of challenging the dominant oppressive powers of his day, and ultimately giving his life. This is the abundant life for which Jesus was born, lived, died, and was resurrected.

Therefore, a consistent pro-life ethic should be concerned with eliminating obstacles to human flourishing in all its forms, as laid out in Scripture. This is similar to what Dr. Martin Luther King Jr. termed "the Beloved Community," in which all people share in the wealth of the earth after racism, poverty, and militarism are abolished via nonviolent principles. We see these cycles of oppression all too clearly in our current society. Generational poverty is extraordinarily difficult to escape. Medical debt destroys futures. Companies forgo paying their workers a living wage, as they seek a larger bottom line and higher pay for the upper management. Our country creates and escalates wars and then refuses to accept refugees from those wars. Children go hungry in our own country, and despite an abundance of calories, there is little nutrition. Pick an area, and they all look bleak: homelessness, hunger, education, the cost of health care, war, imprisonment, climate change, gun violence. These circumstances are all antilife; they directly take away from human flourishing and fulfillment, from that abundant life that Jesus promised and that Dr. King believed was an achievable reality, at least in part, here on earth. They also disproportionately affect people who are already vulnerable, especially the poor and people of color.

Sister Song, a reproductive justice collective made up of women of color, is on the front lines of this intersectional justice work. They center the needs of the most vulnerable, speaking out against a "pro-choice" movement that has largely been led by upper- and middle-class white women such as myself. They name reproductive justice as a human right, per the United Nations' Universal Declaration of Human Rights, and see the primary issue as access, not choice. What good is the individual freedom to make a choice if you cannot access the care to bring that choice to fruition? Sister Song recognizes that marginalized women face multiple, intersecting oppressions that make it ineffective to fight for single issues. White Christians who are inspired by the vision of abundant life for all should center and listen to what groups like Sister Song have to say.

Our world is on a precipice. It is engulfed in war. It is suffering from drought and floods and hurricanes and other natural disasters and extreme weather linked to climate change. It is overburdened with greenhouse gases. It is groaning under the weight of the humans who have mined and fracked oil out of its surface. While those of us in developed countries consume the most energy and produce the most waste, it is people in developing countries who are most at risk from the droughts, floods, and other variations in climate that we have wrought. In considering human flourishing, we must look not just at an individual and her womb but also at our impact on creation and the environment.

A consistent pro-life ethic includes not only an unborn child but its mother, her community, and the world in which she lives. How are these systems set up to support broader human flourishing? For the most part, they aren't—particularly if she is a woman of color or living in poverty. If the high numbers of abortions are distressing to us, then the primary place that we should locate our efforts to reduce them is not with the woman herself, by stigmatizing sex or making abortions more difficult to obtain, but in the social system that surrounds her and supports her. As a nation and a religion, if we say that we value mothers, parenting, and families, then why do we make it so difficult for families to both raise children and provide for themselves as active members in our economic system? This is where we can find common ground with those who are antiabortion—in the formation of and activism toward a pro-life ethic, one that would continue to decrease the rate of abortion.

Additionally, this should lead us to collaborative action in other arenas where life is undervalued or at risk. Pro-life also looks like advocating against the death penalty and supporting workers who demand safer working conditions. Pro-life means making society safe for women by fighting sexual harassment, assault, and abuse. Pro-life means taking steps so that we leave a healthy planet for the generations after us. A broad and consistent pro-life ethic means taking seriously God's action for life, which is ultimately demonstrated in the ministry, death, and resurrection of Jesus Christ. Believing that God will make all things new in the fullness of time does not exempt us from participating in the inbreaking of God's kingdom here and now by working together with those with whom we disagree toward full human flourishing for all people.

Chapter 7
WHERE DO WE GO FROM HERE?

We have examined the history of abortion from the standpoint of society, politics and the law, theology, medicine, and what Scripture and our church bodies do and don't say about abortion. We have tried to reframe and reclaim what "pro-life" means and looks like for a Christian. So where do we go from here?

Fortunately, God has given us different gifts for service to the one body. Some may be called to activism on the political level, while others may be called to have challenging conversations on a personal level. Some will show up at rallies in support of organizations that provide health care for women, and some will walk and pray alongside individuals faced with an unplanned pregnancy. Some will use this opportunity and knowledge to talk about their own abortions or the abortions that happened within their families. What follows are a few action items that you might prayerfully consider.

HAVING CONVERSATIONS
THAT BUILD BRIDGES, NOT WALLS

As with other hot-button issues, talking about abortion in a nuanced and sensitive way with people who disagree is very challenging. Too often, those of us who don the pro-choice label accuse antiabortion advocates of hating women, or at least wanting to confine us to the traditional roles of bearing and nurturing children. On the other side, people accuse those who support a woman's right to choose of supporting the unjustifiable murder of a vulnerable and voiceless human being. I recently saw a comment on social media bemoaning the current state of our society: "Women used to be willing to die for their children." We seem to forget that we are talking about real people and their lives, not just using this as an ideological purity test or an intellectual exercise.

Because of the stridency and tenor of the debate, we forget that most people are in what Katha Pollitt calls the "muddled middle." They're not likely to say much about abortion either way, whether in person or on social media, because their views and feelings on the issue are complex. They identify as "pro-life" but, when pressed, agree that abortion should be available and accessible in situations like rape and incest or the endangerment to the physical or mental health of the mother. They probably aren't as convinced that an embryo has full personhood from the moment of conception but do consider life and potential life as a gift and something of value that should be nurtured and protected. They agree with many of the denominational statements that abortion should not be used as birth control and should be accessed only as a last resort after exploring all other options.

No matter where on the spectrum we find ourselves, we can have constructive conversations if we begin with our points of agreement and common ground. Most of us can agree that abortion should be legal in some circumstances and that it should not be a decision entered into lightly.

I don't know many "pro-life" people who think abortion should be illegal in all circumstances, and I don't know many "pro-choice" people who think abortion is no big deal or something into which a person enters lightly. Do you? These labels tend to divide more than they unite, as it is likely that we have more in common than we think, even if we label ourselves differently.

One way of starting a conversation with people across the aisle from us might be to ask them what they mean when they label themselves "pro-life" or "pro-choice." What does that label mean to them? Rather than challenging someone or trying to argue them into changing their mind with our facts and figures, we can instead listen for the values behind those labels. From that point, we can talk about where those values coexist in desired outcomes: that abortions continue to decrease and that the lives of women, particularly those who are already vulnerable, not be endangered. Surely no reasonable person, even the most passionate pro-life advocate, wants to return to the days of illegal, dangerous abortion providers causing desperate women injury and death. We can spend all day arguing over fetal personhood and women's equality without ever recognizing that ultimately we want similar outcomes.

If we agree on these points, we can work together to support women and their families with discussion of some of the public policies that follow in this chapter or by encouraging each other to take personal action. Through conversations like these, some may realize a calling to get involved with the foster system or become a sex educator for youth. Pro-choice clergy may join a service like Faith Aloud, which provides women with religious and spiritual support for abortion and pregnancy options. We may not agree on everything, but if we can come together on the values that we do share, we can make a bigger difference united rather than divided.

When we talk with other Christians, we should have even more in common. We can agree that we are created in the image of God and that God has a plan of redemption for our broken and fallen world. We can acknowledge that sin and evil are very real things that manifest in all kinds of ways and affect individuals, families, communities, and countries. We share a desire for intact and healthy families to raise up children within communities that support human flourishing.

Unfortunately, so much of our political rhetoric is simplistic and divisive; so these conversations are more and more difficult to have. People assume that if you vote for one party or the other, you feel a certain way about abortion, and, to be sure, there are still single-issue voters out there. It is much easier to be dismissive than to engage one another's concerns. Is there a quicker way to shut down a conversation than by calling someone a baby-killer? It is easier for me to write off religious values that someone else holds dear by flippantly responding, "Well, if your religion is against abortion, then don't get an abortion," than it is for us to have a conversation about protecting the vulnerable and defining who the vulnerable are. It is easier for someone who defines herself as pro-life to accuse those of us who call ourselves pro-choice of being murderers, who would coerce anyone in any kind of difficult situation into getting an abortion, than it is to talk about women as moral agents with bodily integrity who can make tough choices consistent with their values, whether that's to carry a pregnancy to term and keep the baby, put a child up for adoption, or abort.

These conversations are hard and challenging. They are best undertaken face-to-face rather than behind a keyboard. They require in-depth listening and reflecting and trying to stay calm when you feel as if you're being attacked. In a world and culture where facts can be shaped and shifted, it may be wiser to stay away from trying to "prove a point," and instead to listen to the deeper concerns and fears. Then together we can move to our hopes and dreams, to imagining a better, brighter future for women, men, and children toward which we can all work.

ADDRESSING UNPLANNED PREGNANCIES

Let's begin with the worst kind of unplanned pregnancy—that which results from rape. Even some of the staunchest antiabortion advocates agree that women should be allowed access to abortion in cases of rape and incest, so as not to traumatize further the victims of these horrible crimes. No matter how hard we might work to eliminate the economic and social difficulties that contribute to women choosing abortion, there will always be situations when access to abortion may be necessary and should be decided upon by a woman, her family, and her doctor, with minimal government interference. While these tragic cases may be a small minority, this is one place where advocates of abortion rights can frequently find common ground with those who are opposed. Being "pro-choice" is just that: defending a woman's choice in these matters. If a child is conceived during a rape and the mother wants to keep it, then that choice should be respected and supported by a woman's community. Sadly, rape victims are often blamed for their own rapes; they were alone or had too much to drink or did not fight off their attacker. While a lot of advice for avoiding rape is directed toward women, the most important way to prevent rape—and thereby prevent unplanned pregnancies due to rape—is to teach men not to rape.

The first proactive step toward lowering the abortion rate is to prevent unplanned pregnancies from happening in the first place—at least to the best of our ability. Currently, unplanned pregnancies make up about 45 percent of all pregnancies, with higher rates among lower-income women. One hurdle to lowering the rate of unplanned pregnancies is a lack of adequate sex education. In many states, the only acceptable form of public sex education is education that stresses abstinence only. With abstinence-only sex education, young people are not taught how effectively to protect themselves from unplanned pregnancies or sexually transmitted infections, and they may not be able or feel comfortable talking to a parent or another adult figure about this. Furthermore, an emphasis on abstinence for the sake of "purity" (mainly directed toward young women and girls) can be very damaging, particularly for those who have suffered rape or sexual assault. Many young women of my generation were taught that having sex before marriage would leave us like a chewed-up stick of gum or a piece of tape that had lost its stickiness. Abstinence-only education has proven to be ineffective at keeping young people from having sex. Even more troubling, they then engage in sexual activity knowing only what their friends tell them or what they might find from disreputable sources on the Internet. A pro-life ethic that supports the whole human person, including their sexuality, contains access to accurate, balanced sex education—including information about contraception and condoms.

For the time being, the responsibility for contraception primarily falls to women, frustrating as that might be; while there are several options, they are not always easily accessible or affordable. Despite their safety, a prescription for many popular forms of contraception, whether a pill, ring, or other method, necessitates a visit to a health-care provider. Navigating insurance, transportation, the cost of a visit and exam, and the cost of the contraception itself can be challenging and expensive. On top of that, some companies and religious nonprofit organizations refuse to cover the cost of contraception on their health insurance plans for religious reasons, as they can be misconstrued as abortifacients that prevent a fertilized egg from implanting. While there are other health reasons for taking hormonal birth control pills, women, whether married or single, should also be able easily to access effective contraception for its own sake. Health care providers like Planned Parenthood offer a sliding scale for treatment, but we must make it easier to access safe, affordable contraception. With the proven safety of the birth control pill and other methods, they should be offered over the counter and covered by all insurance, including Medicaid. Better yet, access to long-acting reversible contraceptives (LARCs) such as IUDs and implants should be improved. Some states are changing the way Medicaid bills procedures, so that women can get LARCs when they are already at the hospital giving birth, instead of being forced to wait six weeks, at which point they might not return.[1]

In good news, recent studies have confirmed that the abortion rate has continued its decline from the 1990s, dropping 12 percent between 2010 and 2014.[2] While people disagree on the cause, it is worth noting that birth rates have not increased. Rather, the data appear to show that fewer women are getting pregnant. The credit seems to lie with better contraception and access to contraception through programs like the Affordable Care Act, combined with a struggling economy and a lower teen-pregnancy rate.[3] While Republicans identify as the "pro-life" party, data from the early 1990s to the present shows a sharper rate of decline in abortions under Democratic leadership. As this book is being written, the fate of the Affordable Care Act and its contraception mandate hangs in the balance with the election of President Donald Trump. If it is repealed, we may begin to see an uptick in the abortion rate if contraception is harder to obtain.

HEARING THE ABORTION STORIES OF OTHERS

One positive way that the Internet and social media have changed the abortion debate is through the proliferation of women telling their own stories in a way that gives abortion a human face. These stories are often moving and go a long way toward evoking empathy for their situations. Recently blog posts, articles, and speeches have given women platforms to talk about the circumstances that led them to seek abortions. Memoir-style books like Glennon Doyle Melton's *Love Warrior* and Jessica Valenti's *Sex Object* talk openly about the authors' experiences with abortion. Statistics and numbers may tell us much, but hearing an individual's story helps us even more to connect on a human level and to name and address some of the circumstances that lead to a woman choosing abortion.

Whether one is reading other people's stories or sharing one's own, these first-person narratives testify to the complicated nature of choosing abortion and involve concerns about family and romantic relationships, health, economic support, and moral and religious values. Some women struggle with choosing abortion, deciding that it is a difficult but right choice. Some say that they felt a kind of spiritual presence after conception. Some consider it just a bunch of cells. Some women find themselves in the horrific situation of aborting a wanted and planned pregnancy to save their own lives and save their child pain, and consequently mourn the loss of their child. Some women are married and can't afford another child. Some women are single and don't feel they have the support to raise a child. Every situation and relationship is different. These stories give a face and a voice to the statistic that one in every three women will have an abortion by the time she reaches her forties.

Abortion and access to reproductive services affect women across racial lines, socioeconomic lines, and religious lines. Women who belong to churches and denominations that are against abortion are just as likely to get abortions as other women. Both women who are antiabortion and women who are pro-choice get abortions. Both women who vote Republican and women who vote Democratic get abortions. Even if you think you don't, the odds are that you know someone who has gotten an abortion, perhaps even someone in your family.

Telling the story of choosing abortion (or being faced with an unplanned pregnancy, considering abortion, and choosing to give birth) is intensely personal and may not be for everyone. For many women, it can be easier to tell these stories to strangers than to their own family members or friends, out of fear of judgment and condemnation. Especially women who were raised in adamantly pro-life households, churches, and communities may experience cognitive dissonance in choosing to seek an abortion for themselves. Some women and families see their choice as a moral one, even though they are against abortion and seek to limit access for others. This continues a narrative that pits women against women and invites judgment on the most personal aspects of a person's life. If we are being harsh, we might call these people hypocrites, but we can also offer them some grace by acknowledging the complex and difficult scenarios that may lead a woman to go against her deeply held values, particularly when it is in conflict with what her social and religious communities believe.

Not everyone needs to write down their story for the national media, but some reproductive rights organizations and Planned Parenthood chapters collect stories anonymously in order to humanize abortion and reproductive rights. The Tennessee Stories Project is a cooperative effort between Planned Parenthood Middle and East Tennessee and Planned Parenthood Greater Memphis Region. They offer a safe space to share personal stories without risk. As they say on their website, their goal "is to promote a culture of compassion in Tennessee and to strip away the stigma associated with abortion by lifting up the voices of those who have had abortions."

The wider social media campaign #ShoutYourAbortion had a similar goal of combating the shame and stigma of abortion, particularly at a time when abortion rights were being politically eroded in many states. Women were encouraged to share their abortion story on platforms like Facebook and Twitter with the hashtag #ShoutYourAbortion. These kinds of efforts to create space for women to share their abortion stories help people see abortion as a normal part of reproductive health care, as something that their neighbors, their teachers, their mothers and daughters use. It also serves as a counternarrative to the antiabortion story that abortion always victimizes and traumatizes women.

If people view abortion as something that happens to other people whom we can stigmatize as immoral or bad, then limiting it is an easier decision. But this can change when people who are against abortion learn that women who seek abortion are regular women whom they know and love, and that one day there might be a circumstance in which they need access to abortion services themselves.

To me, giving voice to these stories is different from *celebrating* abortion, which is how these types of initiatives are usually perceived by those opposed to abortion. Similarly, movements to tell stories about rape and sexual assault are not a celebration of rape and sexual assault; rather, they humanize the suffering caused by sexual violence and help reduce the shame and stigma. Unfortunately both abortion and sexual violence are common, and we should not turn away from these witnesses. Additionally, more women have shared their experiences around miscarriage and found support and encouragement from others who have walked that same path. Sharing gives a face and a voice to a common experience for women and reinforces that we are talking not about abstractions but about real people. The sheer variety and individuality of abortion stories is moving and powerful, and many testify to the importance of having that safe, legal, and accessible option.

If you drive by any Planned Parenthood office or women's clinic that provides abortion services, you're likely to see protestors berating women who dare to cross the threshold of that clinic. Their shouts and posters with pictures of dead fetuses are intended to shock and shame women, whether they are going in for an abortion or a breast exam. I cannot imagine that being yelled at and called a murderer by a stranger is likely to change anyone's mind. What we can do is listen to and read the first-person accounts of women who have chosen abortion and seek to address the issues that they raise, both in personal relationships and on the broader, systemic level.

SEEKING TO CHANGE SOCIETY

In the world of mainstream feminism, the stated goal for women is equality: equal rights, equal opportunities, equal pay, and so forth. We want equal representation in the Senate and as CEOs of Fortune 500 companies. We have women clergy, women soldiers, and women firefighters. After all, women make up half of the population. But is that all there is to it, simply equal representation within the framework of a world designed by and for men? Or should the goal of feminism be wider and broader, to change that very society that relies on hierarchy, exploitation, and oppression?

The way society is currently arranged, women must control and time their pregnancies in order to advance and be successful in the public sphere. Any professional woman is aware of times in her career when she will be punished, either passively or actively, for getting pregnant and taking time for the physical demands of childbirth and the emotional work of family bonding. Women learn carefully to time their pregnancy announcements to their workplace until after a promotion has been decided. When women are still the primary caregivers for children, they are the ones missing work to pick up a sick child from school. Women who work in the service economy often have to control their pregnancies so that they can afford to take time, as there is currently no federally mandated paid family leave for hourly employees, and any time away from work means no income.

Our broader culture is enslaved to the almighty dollar and to climbing the ladder of power and privilege, usually represented by a larger paycheck. Jobs that involve caretaking, whether of children, the elderly, or the disabled, have pitifully low compensation. Our late-capitalist economy is still set up for men to be the primary movers and shakers in the public sphere, while childraising and elder care fall disproportionately to women, who are then punished and passed over for advancement in the workplace. To be successful, women must be as productive as men, often while still managing the care of their families and households. The bulk of unpaid labor—cooking, cleaning, and childcare—falls to women. While this is essential to the functioning of society, it prevents women from doing other things.

But what if this were not so? Yes, we can focus on smaller political efforts to reduce the number of unwanted pregnancies and abortions by improving sexual education and access to birth control; but ultimately we need to reimagine society completely, from a feminist perspective. As Charles Camosy, in his book *Beyond the Abortion Wars*, sums up Sidney Callahan's essay "Abortion and the Sexual Agenda: A Case for Pro-Life Feminism," a true feminist society would not conform to male models and ideas of social equality but would "make room for the biological reality of women."[4] Rather than accepting the male view of pregnancy as a disease or burden, a pro-life feminist view argues that "pregnancy is an exercise in life-giving power that men can never know."[5]

I would love to live in the society that Callahan describes, but we are not there yet, not even close. This pro-life feminist agenda is one that I feel many Christians could get behind because of the ways in which it privileges life and the uniquely feminine power of giving birth to new life. While pregnancy and childbearing and childraising are primarily a burden on women, no matter how desired or welcomed, this is "precisely because our social structures have been designed by and for human beings who cannot get pregnant."[6] In this way, Camosy takes Callahan's points to argue that abortion rights are primarily beneficial to men, by leaving unchanged the patriarchal social structures that perpetuate an "individualist, disconnected, hierarchical, autonomy-focused view of the person."[7] In contrast, a feminist social structure would be more communal, connected, egalitarian, and just.

A society structured in this way would look vastly different from our current culture, where, for so many of us, work is at the center of our lives. This new culture would be communal and collaborative rather than competitive and consumerist, more relational and less transactional. Our meaning and identities would be found in our families and communities rather than our jobs, and there would be time and space for rest and recreation, or what we might call sabbath. A slower pace of living would allow for deeper relationships and mutual delight in one another, rather than trying to figure out how someone can benefit me. This society would be inclusive of the rhythms of family life and those with physical or mental differences.

I find very persuasive and appealing Callahan's argument that we need a more inclusive focus on justice, on the vulnerable, and on the intrinsic value of human life, and his call for more empathy and nonviolence in rejection of male aggression and destruction.[8] This is consistent with our Christian understanding of "pro-life" and consistent with the feminist tenets that I hold.

I think the church can do a lot to live out this feminist vision for a world in which the life-giving power of women is celebrated. After all, our Savior was born of an unwed teenage mother who was part of a religious minority living in an oppressive empire. Mary, the mother of Jesus, literally bore God in her womb. Is there any better feminist icon of connecting with and privileging the vulnerable?

That vision of the world, one which we believe was partially inaugurated by Jesus' resurrection, is already but not yet. We must also acknowledge the very real social and economic impact that an unwanted pregnancy has, especially on those who are most economically vulnerable. In our current situation, a woman's quality of life is directly tied to her ability to choose when and with whom to have children. This can be managed to some degree with contraception, but there is still no fail-safe, reversible method. As moral actors, women should be able consciously to choose to end that pregnancy if the personal, physical, mental, and economic costs are simply too high.

This raises the question of how much "choice" a woman really has if our present social structures "force women to choose between (1) honoring their roles as the procreators and sustainers of the earliest stages of human life and (2) having social and economic equality with men."[9] For some women, the "choice" is not just equality with men, but sheer survival. A single mother with two children working a minimum wage job is trying to keep a roof over her head and food on the table, not striving to sit at the head of the boardroom table, and yet she too might be faced with an unplanned pregnancy that threatens to push her over the edge.

While feminism talks a lot about women, women's rights, and women's place in society, men would also benefit from a more feminist society. Though things are improving slowly, men's value and self-worth still primarily come from their ability to provide financially for their families. Often this comes at the cost of being disconnected physically and emotionally from their family lives. We see this when strangers ask a father grocery-shopping with a child if he is babysitting today—as if spending time with one's own child is not an expected part of parenting. A capitalist patriarchal system reinforces toxic masculinity and strict gender norms, inhibiting men from expressing emotions, which can lead to unhealthy coping mechanisms and addictions. Men who believe that they must not be perceived as "weak" often overcompensate by showing their dominance, through sex or violence or flaunting status through possessions. Feminism frees men from this destructive system, which equates their worth with what they can produce.

Our ultimate goal is a world and a society in which all life is valued and welcomed, in which women are never forced to choose between socioeconomic security and a pregnancy, and in which the power of women to incubate and give birth to new life is recognized for the power it is. Smashing the system of patriarchal capitalism will both benefit women and cause life and potential life to be treated with empathy and nonviolence within a broadly pro-life framework.

SUPPORTING WOMEN AND FAMILIES

While a society and culture in which all life is valued may seem far away, there are public policies that support women, children, and their families for which we can advocate here and now. Among developed countries, the United States consistently ranks toward the bottom in areas like maternal health and infant mortality, with less healthy conditions concentrated in poorer, Southern states like Alabama, Mississippi, and Louisiana.[10] Oddly, some of these states are the most restrictive when it comes to reproductive rights. If we claim to be concerned about women and their children, disparities in health care must be reduced, particularly in poor, rural areas and places mostly populated by people of color.

In contrast to other industrialized nations, the United States offers no federally mandated paid family leave in the event of a birth or adoption, though the 1993 Family and Medical Leave Act (FMLA) mandated a twelve-week unpaid leave. In Slovenia, fathers may take twelve weeks of paid leave, and in the United Kingdom, forty weeks of paid leave are offered. For many families, giving birth is just too costly in terms of missing work, prenatal health care, and the actual birth itself. Although robust social policies like those in many Scandinavian countries have not been shown to reduce the rate of abortion, putting in place policies like these would show that we do value families and parenting and want to support them.

Our expansive pro-life ethic must address how we can better support families in their current incarnation. Whether we like it or not, the shape of the average American family has changed quite a bit over the past fifty years. The shifting gender roles and the demands of our current economy mean that the typical American family is no longer a father working outside the home and a mother who manages the household and children. For many families, a single income is not enough to support another adult and children, and these economic pressures lead women to consider abortion in the case of unplanned pregnancies. According to the Guttmacher Institute, in 2014, 59 percent of abortions were obtained by women who had already had one birth.[11]

If we want to encourage women to carry a child to term, she must have a way to support her children economically. Right now, women make up two-thirds of minimum-wage workers, and more than half are over the age of twenty-five and without a spouse upon whose income they can rely.[12] These jobs don't provide for paid leave when children are sick or otherwise out of school, and the low wage means that a woman with two children working full time will annually still make $4,500 below the poverty line. Raising the minimum wage would give a raise to nearly half of the working single women of color. We must support families of all shapes and sizes by raising the minimum wage and ensuring equal pay for equal work.

Even for families with financial resources, childcare for children too young for public school is a huge expense, and others rely on other family members to fill the gap. For families who need two incomes, one of those incomes might end up paying for childcare, so families are forced to make tough decisions about remaining in the workforce or raising young children. Leaving the workforce for years to raise children disproportionately affects women, and they often struggle to regain similar positions after taking "time off." Access to prekindergarten programs might help with this issue, in addition to preparing children for school, though recent studies are unclear as to whether there are measurable educational benefits. To complicate matters, many childcare workers make dismal wages and may be sacrificing involvement in the lives of their own children to take care of other people's.

A broad pro-life ethic might also lead to our involvement in the foster system or with adoption. While some pregnant women might consider adoption, it has never been a very popular preference, and the current rate of unmarried white women who offer their baby for adoption is lower than 2 percent.[13] With the decreasing social stigma against single mothers, most women who publicly carry a child for nine months and undergo the pain of childbirth do not see adoption as an attractive option. Rather than being applauded for choosing life over terminating a pregnancy, women who give up a child for adoption face additional judgment. But there are far too many children involved in the foster system who were born to mothers in difficult circumstances and need stable and safe care from adult role models. Pro-life should include caring for the children we already have in our midst, especially those with complicated family relationships or those who have experienced trauma.

A consistent pro-life ethic would be just as committed to supporting families in meaningful and tangible ways as they are in pushing for birth, which can happen on the interpersonal level as well as the policy level. Ideally, the prevailing public witness of pro-life advocates would be offering to babysit for stressed parents or helping a single mother run errands rather than protesting at clinics with abortion services. Churches could provide subsidized childcare for those under the poverty level or summer programs while children are out of school but parents are still working. In mirroring God's action for life, we must work to create a society that actively benefits women, children, and families instead of seeing them as a liability.

CHANGING THE QUESTIONS

Perhaps the most important thing we can do is drop the divisive and increasingly useless labels of pro-life and pro-choice, liberal and conservative, evangelical and mainline. As we've discussed, these labels obscure more than they illuminate, and most people find themselves somewhere in the middle. Furthermore, we need to change the questions that we ask. We can debate all day about whether life begins at conception or implantation or birth, but that doesn't do a lick of good for a woman who needs help.

First, we must stop shaming and stigmatizing women for having sex. Both women and men were created to be sexual creatures. Yet I frequently encounter some version of "if girls would just keep their legs shut . . ." Not only does this diminish our God-given sexuality, it ignores the reality of sexual assault and rape. We also cannot have a society that both stigmatizes single mothers and has a low abortion rate. If we are serious about helping more women choose birth over abortion, we must recognize the struggles and strength of single motherhood and help these women to care for their families. We should not stigmatize women for the choices of men who regularly walk away from unplanned pregnancies.

Engaging in thoughtful conversations helps us recognize the good, the moral, and the noble in the "other side." Too often, we are anything but Christian to our fellow Christians. Those arguing for reproductive rights are written off as murderers and baby-killers, while those who are against abortion are said to hate women, are accused of preferring the unborn to the already-born, and are ridiculed for thinking that a just-fertilized egg is the same as you or me. Those of us who use the label "pro-choice" should admire the conviction and commitment of the "pro-lifers" for the vulnerable and voiceless, including the unborn. Those who term themselves "pro-life" must acknowledge the very real and complicated concerns of women and their families who are struggling to get by in a highly competitive and vicious world and the diversity of reasons women choose abortion.

Our politics, our differing beliefs, and the media seek to divide us, but Christ seeks to unite. When we turn on the news or click on a Facebook link, we are bombarded with polarization, with few nuanced, complex views. For example, when Hillary Clinton announced Senator Tim Kaine as her running mate for vice president, some reproductive-rights activists wrote him off for being "pro-life," even though he had never tried to legislate that belief and had outstanding scores from organizations like Planned Parenthood. What Camosy calls the "corporate/media/political-industrial complex" gets ratings and revenue from covering complicated issues in a way that is simplistic and drives wedges between us.[14] In this particularly divisive time in our nation, Christians and the church could demonstrate a better way. We know that neither party fully represents our Christian tradition and values, and so we must come together to fight for the values we do hold in common.

The most dangerous policies for women and children are those that limit or prohibit abortion access without having measures in place that support families and children. We cannot ban abortion and cut free school lunch. In our states, in our nation, we cannot force women to carry unwanted pregnancies and not provide them with any support. We must work toward measures like equal pay and antidiscrimination laws, paid family leave, and adequate health insurance coverage. We must also come together on other issues of death and violence in our country and world, like the death penalty, war, the ongoing Syrian refugee crisis, and assisted suicide.

In watching the news and participating in the public sphere, we may feel that the loudest voices in the abortion debate do not represent our own more nuanced stance, that the "pro-life" and "pro-choice" labels chafe more than they accurately describe. Our calling as Christians is to something different from the divisive rhetoric of the status quo. We assert that we can be faithful Christians and affirm a woman's right to choose while longing and working for a world in which fewer women find abortion to be the best option. We are called to build bridges, even with those who disagree with us on abortion, and, with the grace of God, to help heal a broken and hurting world. In doing so, may we ask God for the grace and courage to be "pro-life"—all life, everywhere and at every stage.

QUESTIONS FOR REFLECTION AND DISCUSSION

Introduction

1. Are you more comfortable with the term "pro-choice" or "pro-life"? In what ways are these labels helpful? In what ways are they divisive?

2. Does your church talk about abortion? Why or why not? How were your views on the morality of abortion formed?

3. Do you agree that Christianity is typically equated with an antiabortion position? If it is, why do you think this is so? Do you think the Christian faith should be known for certain political views? Why or why not?

Chapter 1: A Brief History of Abortion from Prehistory to Illegality

1. How do you respond to the early church fathers' arguments for "spontaneous animation" or "delayed ensoulment"? Is the status of the fetus's soul important in your thinking about abortion?

2. What impact do you think attitudes toward women have had on beliefs and policies about abortion? How do you feel about church and political policies

on abortion, contraception, and women's health in general being made by men?

3. How does taking "the long view" of sex, contraception, and abortion throughout the millennia affect your thinking about twentieth- and twenty-first-century practices and policies?

Chapter 2: Before and After *Roe v. Wade*

1. Looking at the one hundred years when abortion was illegal in the United States, what conclusions do you draw about access to abortion today?

2. What moral link, if any, do you see between contraception and abortion? Does the "slippery slope" from contraception and abortion to eugenics seem like a real risk to you?

3. From mid-twentieth-century hospital committees to public opinion to policymakers before and after *Roe v. Wade*, what are the limitations and dangers of trying to determine "legitimate" reasons to have an abortion?

Chapter 3: Faith and Fertility in a Changing Culture

1. What social changes do you think most affect women's choices regarding their fertility? How should these social changes influence the church's attitude and our nation's laws on abortion?

2. How do all the advancements in medical technology in recent decades affect our positions on abortion?

3. How are medical technologies used by both antiabortion activists and abortion rights activists to advance their positions?

Chapter 4: What the Bible Does (and Doesn't) Say

1. In general, how does Scripture shape your views on moral questions? How does the Bible provide insight for modern issues and decision making?
2. What Scriptures do you find most relevant to the discussion of abortion?
3. How can you appeal to the Bible to find common ground with Christians who hold different views on abortion?

Chapter 5: Pro-Choice Churches?

1. Does it surprise you that numerous denominations have official pro-choice stances? How do you respond to your own denomination's position on abortion?
2. Why do you think many mainline clergy and denominational leaders are more "liberal" on the issue than their congregants? How should churches seek to reconcile the diversity of viewpoints within their body?
3. What can churches do to minister to women facing unplanned pregnancies, women who have born children into difficult circumstances, and women who have had abortions?

Chapter 6: Reframing Pro-Life and Finding Common Ground

1. What do you think of the definition of "common-sense person"? How do you balance concern for the life of the unborn and concern for the life of pregnant women?

2. What kind of separation is there between your personal beliefs on the morality of abortion and the likelihood of your choosing it for yourself, and a belief in others' freedom of choice and compassionate understanding?

3. How does the inherently tragic element of abortion, similar to the tragic element of divorce, shape your response to people who have had abortions and people who view abortion as murder?

4. How do we promote a "consistent ethic of life" in a world where rape, poverty, patriarchy, racism, stigmatizing judgment, and catastrophic medical circumstances are unfortunate realities?

Chapter 7: Where Do We Go from Here?

1. Imagine you are witness to a heated discussion between someone who insists abortion in every case is murder and someone who believes abortion on demand is an essential right. How could you help establish some common ground in the discussion?

2. If you have heard or read other women's stories of having an abortion, how do their different circumstances—from first-trimester termination of an unplanned pregnancy to an early induction at twenty-four weeks after a devastating diagnosis—affect your thinking about the morality, politics, and justice of access to abortion?

3. How do you think a society absent of patriarchy—a society that took seriously women's bodies, the realities of childbearing, and the good of all people—would promote a consistent ethic of life? How can we work toward such a society?

NOTES

Introduction

1. Leslie Salzillo, "Catholic Nun Explains Pro-Life in a Way That Will Stun Many (Especially Republican Lawmakers)," *Daily Kos*, July 30, 2015, http://www.dailykos.com/story/2015/07/30/1407166/-Catholic-Nun-Explains-Pro-Life-In-A-Way-That-May-Stun-The-Masses.

Chapter 1: A Brief History of Abortion from Prehistory to Illegality

1. Daniel C. Maguire, *Sacred Choices: The Right to Contraception and Abortion in Ten World Religions* (Minneapolis: Augsburg Fortress, 2001), 33.

2. Tertullian, *A Treatise on the Soul*, Chapter XXXVII.

3. Clement of Alexandria, *The Tutor* 2:10.

4. Maguire, *Sacred Choices*, 36–37.

5. Ibid., 35.

6. Augustine, *De genesi ad litteram* 9, 5–9.

7. Thomas Aquinas, *Summa Theologica* I q. 92 a. 1.

8. Katha Pollitt, *Pro: Reclaiming Abortion Rights* (New York: Picador, 2014), 73.

9. Christine Gudorf, "Contraception and Abortion in Roman Catholicism," in *Sacred Rights: The Case for Contraception and Abortion in World Religions*, ed. Daniel Maguire (New York: Oxford University Press, 2003), 69.

10. Maguire, *Sacred Choices*, 124–25.

11. John Calvin, *Commentaries on the Four Last Books of Moses*, in *Calvin's Commentaries* (Edinburgh; repr., Grand Rapids: Baker, 1999), 41–42.

12. Maguire, *Sacred Choices*, 124.

13. Leslie J. Reagan, *When Abortion Was a Crime: Women, Medicine, and Law in the United States, 1867–1973* (Berkeley: University of California Press, 1998), 8.

14. Vicki O. Wittenstein, *Reproductive Rights: Who Decides?* (Minneapolis: Twenty-First Century Books, 2016), 33.

15. Reagan, *When Abortion Was a Crime*, 12.

16. Wittenstein, *Reproductive Rights*, 39–40.

17. Ibid., 40.

Chapter 2: Before and After *Roe v. Wade*

1. Vicki O. Wittenstein, *Reproductive Rights: Who Decides?* (Minneapolis: Twenty-First Century Books, 2016), 44.

2. Ibid., 16.

3. Ibid., 14.

4. Ibid., 13.

5. Ibid., 59.

6. Leslie J. Reagan, *When Abortion Was a Crime: Women, Medicine, and Law in the United States, 1867–1973* (Berkeley: University of California Press, 1998), 14, 138.

7. Ibid., 21.

8. Ibid., 41.

9. Ibid., 59.

10. Ibid., 103.

11. Daniel K. Williams, *Defenders of the Unborn: The Pro-Life Movement before* Roe v. Wade (New York: Oxford University Press, 2016), 159.

12. Sarah Weddington, *A Question of Choice:* Roe v. Wade, *40th Anniversary Edition* (New York: The Feminist Press, 2013), 164.

13. Daniel K. Williams, *Defenders of the Unborn: The Pro-Life Movement before* Roe v. Wade (New York: Oxford University Press, 2016), 203.

14. Katha Pollitt, *Pro: Reclaiming Abortion Rights* (New York: Picador, 2014), 3.

15. Williams, *Defenders of the Unborn*, 207.

16. Wittenstein, *Reproductive Rights*, 91.

17. Ibid., 102.

18. Reagan, *When Abortion Was a Crime*, 250.

19. Molly Redden, "Texas Has Highest Maternal Mortality Rate in Developed World, Study Finds," *The Guardian*, August 20, 2016, https://www.theguardian.com/us-news/2016/aug/20/texas-maternal-mortality-rate-health-clinics-funding.

Chapter 3: Faith and Fertility in a Changing Culture

1. BioWink GmbH, "Clue—Period Tracker," Google Play Store, Vers. 3.3.11 (2017), http://www.helloclue.com (accessed on February 23, 2017).

2. Katha Pollitt, *Pro: Reclaiming Abortion Rights* (New York: Picador, 2014), 81.

3. Ibid., 83.

4. Charles C. Camosy, *Beyond the Abortion Wars: A Way Forward for a New Generation* (Grand Rapids: Eerdmans, 2015), 36.

5. Sarah Zhang, "Why Science Can't Say a Baby's Life Begins," *Wired*, October 2, 2015, https://www.wired.com/2015/10/science-cant-say-babys-life-begins/.

Chapter 5: Pro-Choice Churches?

1. Kathy L. Gilbert, "5 Conferences Join Faith Coalition on Reproductive Rights, Abortion," *United Methodist News*, June 22, 2016, http://www.umc.org/news-and-media/oregon-idaho-takes-up-support-for-rcrc-denied-at-gc2016.

2. Daniel C. Maguire, *Sacred Choices: The Right to Contraception and Abortion in Ten World Religions* (Minneapolis: Augsburg Fortress, 2001), 127–28.

3. United Methodist Church, "What Is the United Methodist Position on Abortion?" http://www.umc.org/what-we-believe /what-is-the-united-methodist-position-on-abortion.

4. "American Baptist Resolution Concerning Abortion and Ministry in the Local Church," http://www.abc-usa.org /wp-content/uploads/2012/06/Abortion-and-Ministry-in-the -Local-Church.pdf.

5. Maguire, *Sacred Choices*, 128–29.

6. Ibid., 131.

7. "United Church of Christ General Synod Statements and Resolutions Regarding Freedom of Choice," *Eighth General Synod*, June 29, 1971, http://d3n8a8pro7vhmx.cloudfront .net/unitedchurchofchrist/legacy_url/2038/GS-Resolutions -Freedon-of-Choice.pdf?1418425637.

8. Southern Baptist Convention, "Resolution on the Partial-Birth Abortion Ban," New Orleans, 1996, http://www.sbc.net /resolutions/26/resolution-on-the-partialbirth-abortion-ban.

9. General Convention, *Journal of the General Convention of . . . The Episcopal Church, Indianapolis, 1994* (New York: General Convention, 1995), 326.

10. General Convention, *Journal of the General Convention*, 323–25.

11. Katha Pollitt, *Pro: Reclaiming Abortion Rights* (New York: Picador, 2014), 101.

12. General Convention, *Journal of the General Convention*, 323–25.

13. Charles C. Camosy, *Beyond the Abortion Wars: A Way Forward for a New Generation* (Grand Rapids: Eerdmans, 2015), 2.

14. Ruth Graham, "The Myth of Abortion Regret," *Slate*, October 13, 2016, http://www.slate.com/articles/double_x /doublex/2016/10/the_myth_of_abortion_regret.html.

15. National Sexual Violence Resource Center, "Statistics About Sexual Violence," 2015, http://www.nsvrc.org /sites/default/files/publications_nsvrc_factsheet_media-packet _statistics-about-sexual-violence_0.pdf.

16. Jill Filipovic, "The Moral Case for Sex before Marriage," *The Guardian*, September 24, 2012, https://www.the guardian.com/commentisfree/2012/sep/24/moral-case-for-sex -before-marriage.

17. Ibid.

Chapter 6: Reframing Pro-Life and Finding Common Ground

1. Charles C. Camosy, *Beyond the Abortion Wars: A Way Forward for a New Generation* (Grand Rapids: Eerdmans, 2015), 12.

2. Ibid., 42.

3. Kim Painter, "Ripped from the Womb? Late-Term Abortion Explained," *USA Today*, October 21, 2016, http://www.usa today.com/story/news/2016/10/21/doctors-trump-wrong-late -abortions/92515324/.

4. Katha Pollitt, *Pro: Reclaiming Abortion Rights* (New York: Picador, 2014), 68.

5. Ibid., 69.

6. Ibid.

7. Ann Furedi, *The Moral Case for Abortion* (London: Palgrave Macmillan, 2016), 102.

8. Jia Tolentino, "Interview with a Woman Who Recently Had an Abortion at 32 Weeks," *Jezebel*, June 15, 2016, http:// jezebel.com/interview-with-a-woman-who-recently-had-an -abortion-at-1781972395.

Chapter 7: Where Do We Go from Here?

1. Michael Ollove, "How Some States Make Effective Birth Control More Available," *PBS Newshour*, November 6, 2016,

http://www.pbs.org/newshour/rundown/states-make-effective -birth-control-available/.

2. David Crary, "Abortions Declining Greatly across Most of US," *Associated Press*, June 8, 2015, https://www.bostonglobe .com/news/nation/2015/06/07/exclusive-abortions-declining -nearly-all-states/DNRxPWSUBMVEq9J7rj6zbI/story.html.

3. Amelia Thomson-Deveaux, "The Abortion Rate Is Falling Because Fewer Women Are Getting Pregnant," *FiveThirty- Eight*, June 12, 2015, https://fivethirtyeight.com/features/the -abortion-rate-is-falling-because-fewer-women-are-getting -pregnant/.

4. Charles C. Camosy, *Beyond the Abortion Wars: A Way Forward for a New Generation* (Grand Rapids: Eerdmans, 2015), 116.

5. Ibid.

6. Ibid.

7. Ibid., 118.

8. Ibid., 116–17.

9. Ibid., 126.

10. Maggie Fox, "U.S. Infant Mortality Rate Stays High, Report Finds," *NBC News*, August 6, 2015, http://www.nbc news.com/health/health-news/us-infant-mortality-rate-still-one -highest-developed-world-n404871.

11. Jenna Jerman, Rachel K. Jones, and Tsuyoshi Onda, "Characteristics of U.S. Abortion Patients in 2014 and Changes Since 2008" (New York: Guttmacher Institute, 2016).

12. National Women's Law Center, "Fair Pay for Women Requires a Fair Minimum Wage," May 13, 2015, https://nwlc .org/resources/fair-pay-women-requires-fair-minimum-wage/.

13. Katha Pollitt, *Pro: Reclaiming Abortion Rights* (New York: Picador, 2014), 186.

14. Camosy, *Beyond Abortion*, 159.

RECOMMENDED RESOURCES

Camosy, Charles C. *Beyond the Abortion Wars: A Way Forward for a New Generation.* Grand Rapids: Eerdmans, 2015.

Church Publishing. *Enriching Our Worship 5: Liturgies and Prayers Related to Childbearing, Childbirth, and Loss.* New York: Church Publishing Inc., 2009.

Maguire, Daniel C. *Sacred Choices: The Right to Contraception and Abortion in Ten World Religions.* Minneapolis: Fortress Press, 2001.

McCleneghan, Bromleigh. *Good Christian Sex: Why Chastity Isn't the Only Option—And Other Things the Bible Says about Sex.* New York: HarperCollins, 2016.

Pollitt, Katha. *Pro: Reclaiming Abortion Rights.* New York: Picador, 2014.

9 780664 262921